Muslim Reformers vs. Fundamentalists

Winner
Contributes to
Diversity & Western Civilization

ISBN: 978-1-7778723-2-8 (Softcover)

ACKNOWLEDGMENTS

I start with those that supported me while I was in Jail. Toshi, Miroslave, Sharon, Frances.

Lorain and Beverley flew from the west to the east.

Man that will not be named.

Frances Flint who's help has been immeasurably instrumental

Thank you all

CONTENTS

CHAPTER 1

AN ISLAMOPHOBE LEARNS FROM IMAMS

They snatched me from the subway car and threw me face down on the platform. I turned to avoid a faceplant. One cop pressed his knee on the back of my thigh; the other cuffed my wrists tight behind my back. This is one of the many minor incidents of my odyssey.

It has brought me to a place where I now more deeply understand not Islam but the fight taking place within the Muslim community. Not the community in Yemen, Qatar, Tajikistan, Pakistan, Afghanistan, Saudi Arabia or Iran, but the Muslim community living and thriving in Canada and all of Western civilization.

Most are not aware this fight is being fought, let alone its significance. Yes, you may have heard whispers that something is going on within Islam. But between driving the kids to soccer practice, paying the mortgage, and putting food on the table, who has time or energy to care about a "foreign" religion?

Once in a while we all need to sit back and relax, recharge our batteries. "Me time." Some people do this by watching combat sports. That is what we have here for you. But this is much more exciting because the stakes are as high as they can get. The victor wins it all. The loser does not come back to play another day.

Team Reform

Professor Irshad Manji and Dr. Zuhdi Jasser are highly touted Muslim reformers who argue that the original Islam was progressive, liberal and democratic. They tell us that mainstream Islam, as practiced in Saudi Arabia, Iran, Egypt, Malaysia, Afghanistan and Pakistan and preached in over 90% of mosques in the West, is perverted, false and wrong. Meanwhile, the mainstream Muslim leadership, who preach in those mosques, label Muslim reformers misguided perverts and apostates.

Dr. Zuhdi Jasser is a social conservative, married with children. He served in the American Navy as a surgeon. He currently specializes in internal medicine and nuclear cardiology. He has been a staff internist to members of Congress and Supreme Court justices and also President of the Arizona Medical Association. He is the author of *A Battle Souls Islam,* a filmmaker, and founder of the American Islamic Forum for Democracy. Since 9/11, he has given numerous interviews which have helped cement his reputation as a leading Muslim reformer.

Irshad Manji began her career as a speech writer in the early 1990s for Audrey McLaughlin, leader of the Canadian NDP party. She is the founder of the Moral Courage Project. She assists major corporations and institutions, private and public, to instill in the workplace a sense of moral courage to speak out against social injustice and to actively promote equity and inclusion. She has authored several books: *Allah, Liberty and Love*; *The Trouble with Islam;* and *Don't Label Me.* Professor Manji has given lectures and interviews throughout the world. She is a social progressive who identifies as a lesbian Muslim. From 2008 to 2015 she was a professor at NYU. Since 2015, she has been teaching at USC in California.

Many champion the Muslim reform movement in the hopes that it will succeed in bringing Islam "into the 21st century" to live in peace and harmony with Western civilization, including the LGBTQ+ community. Others deride the leaders of the Muslim reform movement as well-meaning individuals spinning a fantasy that benefits them enormously by affording them the means to live in ivory towers and ignore certain realities. These skeptics say that living in towers puts the reformers safely above the many consequences of their attempted reform that affect people living closer to the pavement.

Jerk on the Subway

I am one of those people who live close to the pavement. Between 2010 and 2015, I was in jail for a total of three years for misdemeanors relating to Islam, such as "hate crimes," "causing disturbances," "breaching bail," "mischief," and "harassment." One of the crimes I committed during my five-year crime spree took place on a Toronto subway car. I spoke to a Muslim man who had engaged me in interfaith bridge-building dialogue. As he was leaving, he repeated the perfunctory, "I am glad we had this conversation and it was good to meet you."

I responded, "Not nice to meet you and I hate Islam and Muslims." This could be considered not a "nice" thing to say. Some will interpret this as me simply being an ass. But that would be incorrect. At the time, I was of the opinion that asserting "Western" values such as freedom of association and free speech was paramount. But to be so publicly rude! People on the subway who heard this were in shock. As the trial judge remarked, "You could hear a collective gasp." For some strange reason, Canadians are profusely polite, acquiescent and apologetic.

Several times in a line for coffee, I've bumped into someone who then apologized. With a smile, I asked, "Why are you apologizing when it was I who bumped into you?"

With a perplexed expression: "I don't know why. Habit I guess."

In another incident, I was walking out of a locker room and ended up in front of a newly arrived 40-year-old man from Africa. As he and I stepped aside, he apologized. I asked him, "What are you apologizing for?" We had a twenty minute conversation. His understanding was that "apologizing is the Canadian way."

The final reason: I was on a city bus having a cell phone conversation about Prophet Mohammad *PBUH* and his child bride. A man sitting several seats in front of me kept turning around. We were both getting off at Sheppard and Bathurst. He was a bit younger than I and similar in size. On the sidewalk, I approached. I was very aware of his legs and hands. I asked why he kept looking at me.

He looked into my eyes. "Are you not afraid?

"Afraid of what?"

"The police."

I offered to buy him a coffee.

He was a Christian Copt who had only been in Canada for six months. He told me that speaking about Mohammad on a bus in Egypt would get me killed by a mob. If I was lucky, I'd be arrested, tortured and ten years later freed. I explained that in Western civilization we have a right to speak our mind about any subject, including Islam or Prophet Mohammad *PBUH*. He said he would be too afraid to criticize or raise any question about Islam, especially in public. I felt sad that this simple humble Christian man in Canada was living under the fear of Islamic rule and the Muslim mob.

The other reason for my comment on the subway was that I wanted to "stir the pot." I prefer not to go along to get along.

Making the Best of Being in Jail

Since when is being a shit disturber a crime? In Canada in 2015, I was convicted and sentenced to five months for mischief, five months for causing disturbance and ten months for breaching probation. "Keep the peace and be of good behavior" – a total of twenty months' imprisonment. The judge made sure everyone got the message. He made the three sentences consecutive. Violent gun-toting bank robbers who are sentenced to four years for each of ten bank jobs serve them concurrently. That is a total of four years, not forty.

Originally the Crown was seeking AGO consent to lay a hate crime charge, but had to settle for a lesser pound of flesh named "cause disturbance." The disturbance was using language such as "I hate Islam" that disturbed the sensitivities of the passengers, three of whom the prosecutor pointed out were young women wearing the hijab.

One of the biggest challenges in jail is boredom. I had, in the past, tried reading the Quran but found it a boring torture, if there can be such a thing as a boring torture. Other than playing chess, cards and walking in a circle, there is not much to do in jail. So, on a previous stint in the Toronto South Detention Centre (I was there for distributing insulting fliers about Muslims in 2013), I obtained a Quran. This particular Quran was translated by Abdul Yusuf Ali in Lahore, Pakistan in 1948, and was approved by the education ministry of Saudi Arabia. Today, most Qurans, particularly the ones used in schools or by interfaith bridge-building organizations, have softened the language. One Quran introduction stated that they substituted the word "torture" for the word "punish" because "punish" implies meting out a deserved and necessary disciplinary action, whereas "torture" implies inflicting pain on the innocent.

I read this Quran for three to four hours almost every day for eight months. On weekends, the Toronto South Detention Center was in lockdown. I read and copied the Quran for eight to ten hours on those days. I copied the Quran verses with a golf pencil. In prison, a pen or full-sized pencil can be used as a weapon. They are prohibited, as are plastic forks and knives. One jail that I was in briefly, Penetang in Penetanguishene, gave out orange-colored soft rubber spoons. The first time I used one, I thought I was hallucinating.

I lengthened the golf pencil with paper using toothpaste as glue. Then I copied the verses that are or could be considered violent or insidious. I went through the Quran this way three times from beginning to end. Each time, I filled thirty pages on both sides. I discovered that when you carefully and neatly write something out, it gets etched into your mind.

I Was Like Bambi

Many have asked why I have dedicated my life to this cause. It began in 2003. After my bi-weekly hockey game at the downtown Toronto YMCA, I would take a sauna and shower, and usually leave by 11:30 pm. The only restaurant open nearby at that hour was on Parliament Street just south of Dundas on the west side. I did not realize that this establishment catered to local Muslim taxi drivers.

One night, I was in the restaurant chatting with a couple of guys about something or other. Many might need reminding that in 2002, the Ontario provincial Liberals of Dalton McGuinty were considering instituting Shari'ah family courts. It was a big political story at the time. I blurted out as a joke – or so I thought – "But no one really wants Shari'ah to come to Canada."

One of them replied, "All Muslims want to live under Shari'ah."

Another added, "Shari'ah is the law of God. It is the duty of Muslims to bring Shari'ah law to Canada."

I replied, "Come on, guys. You're making a joke. Right?"

The mood in the small dining room changed. These men, who moments ago had been affable and jovial, became somber, almost menacing. One said, "We do not joke about the law of Allah."

I smiled nervously and said, "Okay then." There was no more chit chat.

The next morning, I woke with the same feeling I had gone to bed with. It was worry, perhaps more like foreboding. It kept running in my mind: "Do Muslims really want to turn Canada into a Muslim country? "

My Montreal days in the mid nineties came flooding back. I was receiving chain emails about the brutal plight of women in Afghanistan. Those were the days of dial-up. It was slow and annoying. But I could not remove myself from the chain. I was conflicted with guilt. Here I was living my easy life in Canada while these women were being tortured and I could do nothing. So I put it out of my mind.

Having a Mental Breakdown

I, like most Canadians, did not spend time thinking about Islam or Muslims. That changed in a big way after this restaurant incident in the winter of 2003. Since then, I have had an interest in Islam bordering on obsession.

Looking back, I see I went overboard. "Off the deep end," as they say. Was I using this to compensate for some shortcomings in my life? Sometimes I wonder about that. We all have multiple motives for what we do. That's for a future self-help book.

In the years leading to my crime spree, I radicalized myself. I'd been watching YouTube videos of Imams preaching about how Islam will take over and destroy Western civilization. They said their main weapon was demographics. Imams openly boasted that Muslim women typically have five babies – European women have less than two. "We will replace them." Imam Karim AbuZaid says that demographers predict that by 2050, Islam will be the majority religion in France. Driven further, I read anti-Islam books: Brigitte Gabriel's *Because They Hate;* Ibn Warraq's *Why I Am Not a Muslim;* Paul Sperry's *Muslim Mafia*; Tarek Fatah's *Chasing a Mirage;* Wafa Sultan's *A God Who Hates* and *They Call Me Infidel* and *The Devil We Don't Know* by Nonie Darwish.

Then the world erupted. In 2012, a Christian Copt in California named Sam Bacile expressing his art and opinions - made a 14-minute movie about Islam and the Prophet Mohammad PBUH that portrayed the Prophet in a less than flattering light. He called the film "Innocence of Muslims" and posted it on YouTube. Muslims the world over began calling for his death. Muslims in Egypt, Kenya, and Sudan attacked Western embassies. Muslims protested and rioted in Western capitals.

Did the West finally take a stand and categorically defend Western civilization and its non-negotiable value of free speech? NO! This was driving me out of my mind. I was constantly talking to everyone. "People, are you blind? Don't you see what is happening? We are losing our civilization."

The response was, "Eric, you need to relax," or, "Eric, you need psychiatric help." Then a spike was driven into my heart. Hillary Clinton, then America's Secretary of State, made an official announcement:

> *We absolutely reject this content and message... To us and to me personally, this video is disgusting and reprehensible. It appears to have a deeply cynical purpose to denigrate a great religion and provoke rage.*

Islamophobe on Fire

I went into full kamikaze mode. With the help of a graphic designer, I made the most offensive fliers I could. One side had a cartoon of a pregnant Muslima wearing a full burqa. Her hands over her belly were skeletal, and the caption read: "The other Islamic bomb. *'They are here & breeding. Kill them wherever you find them. 9:5'*" On the other side was a depiction of Mohammad with his nine-year-old wife; a man wearing a turban defecating on blank paper: "*Mohammad Writes the Quran.*"

I handed these fliers out in downtown Toronto's Dundas Square, at mosques, and at Ryerson Campus. I was calling out, "Mohammad was a pedophile; Islam is a satanic religion. I am an artist; this flier is my art." About a week later, I was in handcuffs. So began my journey into the dark criminal world of hate crimes. The Crown did not get AGO consent for "incitement to commit genocide" so I was charged with your garden variety "willful promotion of hate," as well as "incitement to hate." I was released from jail eleven months later, time served. I was serving the last three weeks of a probation order during the subway incident I described above.

Back to the ten-month sentence for breach. Breaching probation is usually fifteen days to one month. I appealed the sentence. At this point I had served twelve of my twenty months. The High Court Crown agreed to bail, pending the appeal.

Three months later November 13th, 2015, France was attacked by misunderstanding Muslim terrorist who shot 500 killing 140

That night, I went to Dundas Square. After two hours of raging and howling and debating, and being punched and kicked by the mob, I was in handcuffs again.

A witness told the police that I said, "I want a gun to shoot and kill all Muslims." I was charged with breach of bail and cause disturbance. The AGO soon gave consent to charge me with incitement to commit genocide.

After ten months, we finally had the preliminary hearing. A prelim takes place only for indictable offences. A judge hears witness testimony and views all the evidence. All this is done under cross examination by the defense lawyer. The judge then rules whether to dismiss or commit to trial.

The judge said, "It seems to me that the Crown is 'shoe-horning' Mr. Brazau into a crime. I find the witness very unreliable." He went on to explain that a preliminary judge cannot base his decision on the credibility of the witness, and that other than this one witness, the Crown had no case. In his opinion, the judge stated, "This case has no merit." However, because of this one witness, he had to refer the case to trial.

Wind on My Face

In ten months, I had been denied bail three times. This judge gave me hope. Five days later, I appeared before him. Two hours after he heard the arguments, I was summoned from the basement dungeon of Toronto Old City Hall. As he started to go through his decision, my heart began to sink. My lawyer gave me a look. The judge went through all the reasons why he should deny me bail. I was feeling despondent. But then he gave the reasons why he should grant me bail. I willed myself not to hope. And then it happened; he granted me bail. The Crown, which was personally invested in this case, was very upset.

Three weeks later, my lawyer told me the presiding Superior judge wanted this case to go away. He suggested the Crown come to a resolution, a deal.

Oddly, the Crown told my lawyer that if I did not take the deal – time served – and opted for trial, she would bring a motion to revoke my bail on the grounds that the preliminary judge had made an error, and that I was a danger to public safety and should be incarcerated… So if I pled guilty, I would not go back to jail, but if I took it to trial to prove my innocence, I would become a danger to society and the Crown would attempt to pull my bail.

The thought of going back to jail for another six months until trial... In February 2017, I pled guilty to breach of bail and cause disturbance. The judge sentenced me to ten months' time served plus one day. I was taken into custody and strip searched. I waited in a bull pen for six hours. I was then driven to the Toronto East Detention Center, processed, then released.

Suffice it to say, the jail period of my life ended in November of 2016. I continued to engage in certain anti-Islam activities, but I was careful to stay far away from crossing any lines. In July of 2018, however, my life took a drastic change.

On July 22, in a place known as Greektown on the Danforth, a Muslim man shot fifteen females, killing two of them. A feature of Greektown is the Alexander the Great parquet, which is similar to a European plaza. It has an ornate water fountain and a statue of

Alexander the Great, and is bordered by an ice cream store, a café and a souvlaki shop. In the immediate vicinity are 25 restaurants with sidewalk patios. Most girls wear flowing summer dresses. Ten-year-old Juliana Kozis came with her family to eat ice cream. She was killed, as was 18-year-old Reese Fallon. Another woman was left a paraplegic.

It was obvious to me that this was an Islamic jihadist attack. The shooter took a bus from his 90% Muslim neighborhood, Thorncliffe Park, to a 90% white Christian neighbourhood that is surrounded by five churches.

Within twelve hours of the shooting, the media was promoting the narrative that the shooter was suffering from "mental health issues." This mental health theory came from a highly polished press release put out by Mohammed Hashim, who is known in Canada as the preeminent Muslim media relations specialist. The mental health narrative was solidified by many interviews with the shooter's parents.

Accidental Baptism

Within 24 hours, Toronto police announced that the shooting was not terror related. How could they know this so quickly? It seemed this was a political announcement to quell the anti-Islam sentiment that was beginning to grow. The anti-Islam sentiment became especially rampant when it was revealed that the mosque the shooter attended in Thorncliffe Park had recited verses and prayers about killing Jews and Christians.[1] Many people suspected that the police had quickly

1 https://news.acdemocracy.org/thorncliffe-mosques-supplication-slay-them-one-by-one/

suppressed this statement to maintain public order and inter-religious cohesion.

The Alexander parquet became a makeshift memorial. Over the next five days, it was packed with people. The mainstream media was in constant attendance. On the ledge of the fountain people placed pictures of the girls, flowers and stuffed animals, and messages about peace and love. Some messages called for sympathy for the shooter and his family. In attendance from day one was a group of twenty or so Ahmadiyya Muslims, who wore matching blue T-shirts and carried large signs that read *"Love for all – Hate for None."* I decided to attend holding a sign that brought attention to the Islamic element that for some mysterious reason was being ignored. People did not like my sign. "You are not welcome here," they were yelling. A scuffle ensued and I was pushed into the fountain. The crowd applauded and laughed. The police, who saw the incident, told me that if I did not leave the vicinity, I would be arrested. I asked why the man that had pushed me into the fountain was not being arrested. They said if I insisted on pressing charges against him, they would press charges against me for causing a disturbance. I was still on probation and would definitely have been made to appear the next morning in bail court. So I left.

The next day, the media from Europe to the Middle East was buzzing with this story. One media outlet had captured a picture of me in the fountain on my back still holding my sign, which read *"CBC Presents Little Mosque on the Prairie/Two Dead Girls in Greek Town."* Ninety percent of the comments supported and even advocated for violence against insensitive, boorish people like me.

I had thought free expression was a non-negotiable pillar of Western civilization. But no civil rights group came to my defense. I am not saying they should have defended my statement, but they should have defended my right to make a statement. I was very confused and deeply saddened by this reaction. Was I losing my sanity, or was the population going insane? After a few moments of doubt, I concluded it was they and not me who were insane. If we do not have absolute freedom to express our thoughts, we are not a free people. Why did Canadians sacrifice their lives in WW1, WW2 and Korea to defeat communism and fascism, if not to defend our way of life? It crept into my mind that maybe they were not insane, but cowards.

The next day, I read a tweet by NCCM (National Council of Canadian Muslims):

> *Violence is not the answer. Islam forbids vigilante justice. This man's views, while repugnant, are permissible in a free democratic country that values free speech.*

Hum?? The Canadian Civil Liberties Association had not issued any statement. But a Canadian Muslim organization was defending the rights of Eric Brazau, notorious Islamophobe and convicted hatemonger? I, as well as others on the right, associated NCCM with CAIR in America, an unindicted co-conspirator in the Holy Land Foundation trial.[2] Was I wrong about NCCM? Was I wrong about Islam? At least, was I wrong about the Islam in Canada? I pride myself on my ability to think rationally and critically. I am a harsh critic of those who do not.

---

2 https://archives.fbi.gov/archives/news/stories/2008/november/hlf112508

That fountain was my baptism, my rebirth. I erased from my mind everything I thought I knew about Islam.

From that time on, I dedicated myself to learning what North American Imams, scholars and literature are teaching about Islam. No longer would I learn about Islam from "radical" Imams in Iran or Saudi Arabia. That included my understanding of the Quran.

This book is my effort to make amends for my past indiscretion, or as some will say, foolish, harmful behaviour. I highlight and juxtapose the voices of the two sides of the Islam debate in an effort to understand and appreciate how these voices – reformer and mainstream fundamentalist – are contributing to the cultural enrichment of Western civilization.

This book will help Christians, Jews, agnostics and atheists sitting at interfaith bridge-building tables gain a contextualized understanding of the richly conceptualized tapestry that underpins the ethos of Islam.

This book will also be of immense value to people suffering from Islamophobia. How? After reading this book, they will more likely accept the reality that there are strong, definitive leading Muslim voices that clearly state not what Islam could be but what it is. It will also help them understand the motives of those who are "perverting" the *true* message of Prophet Mohammad *PBUH*. Finally, those who advocate increasing support for the Muslim community now have access to vital insider knowledge that will clarify their understanding.

A wise man once said,
what people do not want to talk about,
for that reason alone, is what we must talk about.

CHAPTER 2

A MUSLIM IS NOT ISLAM, NOR IS ISLAM A MUSLIM

In this chapter we will consider whether any particular Muslim is an authentic representative of Islam. Generally, in the minds of Westerners, religion is a private affair and that makes it not their business. However, after every Muslim jihadist attack, many Westerners have something to say about Islam and Muslims. We will explore what that is and why.

After Every Attack, Messaging Is Fast and Furious

Inevitably, after every jihad attack committed by someone who identifies as Muslim, the mainstream and alt media will spin one of two familiar narratives. "This Muslim killed these people because his religion Islam is evil," or, "This man is known to have mental health issues and does not represent the peaceful religion of Islam." Repeating these two polarizing narratives does little to uncover whatever unconscious bias has been drummed into society.

When people are asked why they believe Islam is either this or that, their answer is usually, "Because everybody knows." When challenged to provide the information that supports their opinion, they react as if they are under attack. They themselves then engage in *ad hominem* attacks. I have experienced this from both sides, from those who are pro- and those who are anti-Islam. When they feel their opinion is challenged, they become personally insecure.

Most people allow themselves to be persuaded by the "good people" who are in positions of authority. One might even say they have unconsciously accepted a form of authoritarianism. This manner of thinking can dull the intellectual robustness of a population. It encourages a "lazy mind" and "sloppy thinking."

Some might say, "Ah… so what? Sloppy thinking is no big deal." But would you set out on an ocean voyage with a captain who was sloppy with his sea charts, and a crew that was often drunk and insubordinate? No one boards a ship merely hoping the voyage will not end in catastrophe. They require assurance from experience. Western civilization is our one and only ship being guided through time.

Accepting Logical Fallacies

If you had an unpleasant experience with a person in an elevator who identifies as a Buddhist, it would be nonsensical to conclude that Buddhism is therefore an unpleasant religion.

Similarly, no one Muslim speaks for Islam, be they pleasant or unpleasant. Professor Irshad Manji and Dr. Zuhdi Jasser are two pleasant people who speak for the Islam Reform Movement They believe in and promote a version of Islam that embraces Western values and sensibilities.

At the same time, there are other Muslim voices in the West who promote a return to an Islam that strongly rejects Western values and sensibilities.

That brings us back to the importance of appreciating that what a Muslim tells us Islam is could be what Islam is, but that is not necessarily so. Similarly, a non-Muslim could say something about Islam that is false. But that is not necessarily so. One can be a member of a particular religion and misunderstand its doctrine. We can be sure that many communists misunderstand some of the finer points made in the Communist Manifesto. The same can apply to Muslims and Islam.

Professor Irshad Manji and Dr. Zuhdi Jasser

Professor Irshad Manji and Dr. Zuhdi Jasser tell us there are two versions of Islam: the "mainstream" version preached at Friday prayer in most mosques, and the original authentic liberal progressive version.

In this book, I use the word "mainstream" in the same way Professor Irshad Manji does: to refer to the Islam practiced and embraced by 97% of mosque-going Muslims.

It is worth pointing out that, although Manji and Jasser have large followings in the non-Muslim world, as well as in the secular and Muslim LGBTQ+ communities, the mainstream Muslim community either totally ignores them or treats them with contempt. Both have been threatened by members and leaders of the Muslim community, overtly and covertly. Dr. Jasser said that once at Friday prayer, the Imam said, "There is a traitor among us." Dr. Jasser knew the comment was directed at him.

Irshad Manji once had to cancel a speaking engagement in Indonesia at the insistence of the police, who were overwhelmed by a Muslim mob shouting for her death. There have also been several incidents in Europe where her speaking engagements were cut short by angry Muslims storming the stage.

Manji and Jasser are fond of regaling readers and listeners with their personal experiences. Since they are pleasant people that accept Western values, non-Muslims prefer to hear their version of Islam. Some argue that expressing this bias marginalizes and otherizes Muslims who have an Islamic experience that is different but true to themselves.

Political Islam Is a Danger

According to the Islamic doctrine and the teachings and lectures of past and current Imams and scholars, Islam is a complete system that regulates man's affairs on all levels. It dictates what hand you eat with, what foot you enter the bathroom with, criminal and civil law, banking, inheritance, child custody and everything else.

Any ideology that controls civic and penal law, banking and education is *ipso facto* a political system. Jasser and Manji continuously talk about "political" Islam, as though it were somehow separate from Islam as a whole. This leaves me confused.

Hizb-ut-Tahrir is an Islamic group that promotes a world caliphate (kingdom). It was established in 1953 and is active in fifty countries, but is particularly well entrenched in Canada, America, Australia, and Central Europe. Its headquarters are in London, England.

This Islamic group is estimated to have ten to fifteen million members worldwide. It shuns the Western political system in favor of establishing a parallel Islamic society governed by Shari'ah. It has published detailed books on every conceivable aspect of administering an Islamic nation, including both criminal and civil judiciary, birth certificates, licensing, garbage removal, water sanitation and public transport, all in a manner that is Shari'ah compliant. It is focused not on subverting or infiltrating Western governments but on assuming power once Western governments fall or are overthrown.

IERA is a Sunni dawa'h (proselytizing) organization that has global reach, as does Bilal Philips's Online University. These are organizations with the highest level of professionalism and seemingly limitless resources. Both offer free online training courses. IERA teaches Muslims how to effectively convert people to Islam. The online university trains Muslims to become Imams.

In 2019, IERA in Britain visited 34 universities 51 times. They also gave 1200 training lectures in 44 countries. They have a working relationship with mosques and have developed 22 dawa'h teams in 13 cities. IERA World Initiative has created 67 dawa'h teams and graduated 36 specialists.

As of 2021, Bilal Philips' online university had 150,000 graduates with advanced accredited degrees in Islamic studies. Bilal Philips, a Sunni Imam, is quoted as saying:

> *Islam is a moral message and to implement that message might require weapons. That is why we have jihad. But spilling blood and acquiring lands is not the objective of jihad.* [3]

Many North American, European and Australian Muslim organizations are closely linked to and influenced by a handful of other organi-

3 *https://youtu.be/-nu7m4oEL4M*

zations, all of which openly aspire to implement Shari'ah rule over every nation. However, Dr. Jasser and Professor Manji do not agree with these aspirations. Their organizations have come out in strong support of Western liberal values and the separation of religion and state.

CEM, the Council of European Muslims, is an umbrella group that comprises the global Muslim Brotherhood in Europe. Its current President is Abdullah Benmansour, alleged to be a long-time leader of the Muslim Brotherhood in France. CEM has its headquarters in Brussels and has had some success in positioning itself as a "dialogue partner" for the EU and other important institutions. CEM has also spawned numerous other organizations, including the European Council for Fatwa and Research (ECFR) and the Federation of Muslim Youth and Student Organizations (FEMYSO).

GISN, the Global Imams and Scholars Network, consisting of seven international scholarly councils, has developed a historic charter for Western Muslim leaders, outlining a general set of principles. The British Board of Scholars and Imams (BBSI), the Australian National Imams Council (ANIC), the European Council of Imams, the Canadian Council of Imams (CCI), the North American Imams Federation (NAIF), the United Ulama (senior scholars) Council of South Africa, and the Ulama Council of New Zealand have all come together to collaborate on mutually beneficial work.

> *The Global Imams and Scholars Network aims to share knowledge and promote traditional and orthodox principles and the message of Islam and preserve the Islamic identity for Muslims living in the West. [SEO description]*[4]

4 *https://muslimmatters.org/2022/05/11/the-global-imams-scholars-charter-the-global-imams-scholars-network/*

In contrast, Muslim reformers contend that Islam is a religion that is not traditional and orthodox but progressive and liberal. Dr. Jasser and Professor Manji advocate reinterpreting or eliminating certain verses in the Quran that may be deemed pugnacious. Mainstream Muslims view such an idea as desecrating the Word of *Allah SWT* and an insult to Prophet Mohammad *PBUH.*

American ISF – Islamic Scholarship Fund – claim on their website that, since 2009, they have awarded $1.9 million in scholarships and grants and have helped place American Muslim scholars in positions that impact public policy and opinion in media, film, law, government, and more.

All the above mainstream Muslim organizations agree on several basic principles:

1. It is the duty of all Muslims to strive, within their ability, to establish Shari'ah law.
2. It is the duty of all Muslims to forbid evil and promote good, if possible, with their hands.
3. Islam is the only permissible religion.
4. Non-Muslims are to be subjugated by Muslims and Islam.
5. Homosexuality is punishable by death.
6. Women need permission to leave the home and must be covered.
7. Punishment for apostasy and blasphemy is death.

Following are the closing statements of the Council of European Muslims (CEM) General Assembly that was held in Istanbul, Turkey from 19th-22nd May 2022 with the participation of representatives of member organizations from across Europe, along with a number of distinguished guests.

> *We call on European Muslims to strengthen their affiliation with their Islamic religious and European national identity, and to work to pass on this affiliation to future generations.*
>
> *The assembly agrees on more coordination between member organizations within the framework of the orientations, principles and values of the Council of European Muslims.*[5]

Do all Muslims agree with the principles and values of CEM? We do know that the preponderance of mosques in the West are under the umbrella of the CEMGA. It follows that Imams in the West will preach the values of CEMGA in their mosques and that members of these mosques will be influenced by the Imams that preach there.

---

5 *https://eumuslims.org/en/media-centre/press-releases/closing-statement-council-european-muslims-general-assembly*

CHAPTER 3

ISLAM IS NOT MONOLITHIC: CONTROVERSY IN DIVERSITY

In this chapter we will learn to appreciate the diversity within Islam that demonstrates the importance of the similarities that tie them together.

An apple, banana and orange are different. But when you compare them to a stick, they are the same.

Certain Islamic movements or strands of Islam that are sweeping regions of America, Europe and Africa are labeled by reformers, Western academics and mainstream media as not representative of the "true" Islam. However, some influential Imams and scholars in the West say that these strands do represent the "true" Islam, or at a minimum, elements of the "true" Islam.

Sunni Islam that is sweeping Africa, Europe, North America, Asia and Australia is divided into four schools of thought: Shafi'i, Hanbali (Hanbaliyyah), Maliki and Hanafism. These different schools contribute to the diversity within Islam. However, to most non-Muslims and many Muslims, these differences are of no great consequence. Some of the differences include disagreements about:

- Where to place the hands during prayer.
- Whether the necessary number of Friday prayers is 3-12 or 40.
- Whether women can lead women in prayer.
- Whether seafood is permissible.
- Whether women are allowed to show the face and hands in public.
- Whether the number of authentic aHadith [aHadith indicates plural] books is five or six.

It is often said that all religions are the same. In one sense, it is true that all religions are the same simply because they are religions. But their differences are what define them. There is a reason Islam is not Buddhism and Buddhism is not Christianity. These differences are paramount to members of these religions. The differences make all the difference.

Similarities that Unite Shia and Sunni

Sunni Muslims elected their leader after the death of Prophet Mohammad *PBUH*. Shia Muslims thought it was a hereditary title. Shia Muslims believe that Imams are sinless saints and venerate their graves. Sunni view this as a major transgression akin to idol worship. However, both Shia and Sunni see it as a religious obligation to eliminate all other religions and ideologies – including each other – and establish supremacy and dominance of Shari'ah rule.

Both believe that when Maddie (savior) arrives he will bring Justice and righteousness to the world and only Islam will be accepted. Both pray five times a day, grow beards and trim mustaches. Both believe in Satan and Angels and in the Oneness of God.

Prominent Muslim leaders make the case that a united Muslim community would be in a more favorable position to bring the blessings of Islam to all Western nations.

There is diversity within the Muslim community regarding commitment to implementing Shari'ah. Some Muslims do not desire Shari'ah but would accept it if it were imposed. There are Muslims who would sacrifice their lives as jihadists to impose the blessing of Islam upon all mankind. There are also those who will not sacrifice themselves, but do support those who will.

Regionally, there is also diversity. For example, in some regions, the percentage of Muslims that are eagerly willing to sacrifice themselves in a suicide jihad mission can be as low as 5%, in others as high as 30%. Meanwhile, Muslim reformers say suicide jihadist terror attacks go against the teaching of the original Islam.[6]

Strength in Diversity?

Right-wingers ask sarcastically whether diversity is really strength. How did this phrase become a truism? They say if diversity were strength, then people would know it to be true, and government institutions, academia and the media would not need to be constantly shoving it down our throats.

---

6 https://www.pewresearch.org/search/suicide+bombing+support

No one, including Canadian Prime Minister Justin Trudeau, a champion of diversity, has clearly explained why diversity and ever more diversity is strength. But in fairness to Prime Minister Trudeau, no one has ever directly asked him this question expecting an answer.

Let us construct three scenarios in which diversity is not strength:

1. Should a chain supporting a crane or some great weight be made of uniform links of the strongest metal, or should the links be diverse in size, made with a diversity of materials?
2. Should the ball bearings in a wheel be all the same, or should there be a variety of sizes and shapes.
3. A nuclear power station is going into critical meltdown. You can choose one of two groups to attempt to prevent this. One diverse group of ten people contains two nuclear engineers, three clowns, two bartenders, and three humanities professors. In the second group, all ten are nuclear engineers.

Let us construct two scenarios in which diversity is strength:

1. The ice cream shop offers 91 diverse flavors?
2. The engineers approached the solution from a diversity of perspectives.

In Canada, the Liberal government of Justin Trudeau is allocating considerable resources to eliminate "wrong thinking" concerning immigration, multiculturalism, diversity, and most particularly Islam. It is important to note that NCCM (whose CEO Mustafa Farooq advocated for Montreal, Ottawa and Edmonton to become Shari'ah mini-states) and CCI (whose leading scholar Imam Yousuf Badat, according to Dr. Jasser, endorsed a Muslim supremacist manifesto by al-Qaradawi) are lead advisors on these projects.

Right-wingers say Islamic leaders spew a constant stream of hate. YouTube videos are rife with North American Imams saying, "Homosexuals are perverts;" "Hating Jews is a Muslim's religious obligation;" "There are only two genders," and so on. Toronto Dawa'h Centre, distributes a book at Dundas Square titled *Women in Islam*: "Women should be beaten only for discipline."[7] Many of these books distributed by the dawa'h group over the past ten years contain the sentences, "O! Allah give us victory over the disbelieving people," and "O Allah, destroy the disbelievers." (*Muslim Prayer Hand Book, Clear your Doubts about Islam, 24 Hours with the Prophet, Accepted Dua*)

Right-wingers and Islamophobes will say this proves there are Muslim fanatics in Toronto who are willing to sacrifice themselves in a jihad suicide attack. This is false. The existence of these books proves nothing other than jihad is possibly being propagated in Toronto. It is also possible even probable that the number of Muslims that will act upon these teachings are a minority.

Muslim reformers like Dr. Jasser and Professor Manji would like to amend away these Islamic writings and teachings. Many non-Muslims support their efforts. But the Canadian government since the 1970s, including Prime Minister Justin Trudeau and the present-day Liberals, are committed to inclusion, tolerance, acceptance and diversity. How then is it possible to exclude any Islamic belief? After all, how does this align with the idea of being "accepting of all cultures and values?" Do human rights advocates wish to deny mainstream Muslims the right to manifest their culture and religion as they like? The Canadian government, through various legislative acts such as the

7 https://learningislam.ca/women-in-islam/

Canada Multicultural Nation Act (1971), the Canadian Human Rights Act (1977), the Employment Act (1986) and the Multiculturalism Act (1988) is committed to promoting non-white, non-European minority people and their cultures. Therefore, the minority Muslim culture will be promoted until it becomes the majority – or at least until it is not a minority. As mandated by the Multiculturalism Act R.S.C., 1985, c (4th Supp).

The Need to Understand

Only in the last four decades has Western civilization become obsessed with not misunderstanding those who identify with Islam. Some ask what quantity of resources the West is devoting to the issue of Islam. What is the return on investment? Is the upside of Muslim diversity worth the cost? Others deem such questions inappropriate.

People who ask these questions also say it is reasonable to assume that if Islam did not exist in the Western world, the fight for the soul of Islam would not be taking place in the Western world. Such statements are considered inappropriate because they go against the narrative that diversity is strength. Others argue that questioning whether diversity is strength weakens the strength of diversity.

CHAPTER 4

THE MUSLIM PROGRESSIVE REFORM MOVEMENT: DR. ZUHDI JASSER

We begin by looking in detail at Dr. Zuhdi Jasser's book *A Battle Souls Islam*. However, equity demands that we also hear the voices of the Muslim community that disagree with Dr. Jasser. This gives us a contextualized understanding that is not influenced by preconceived notions, unconscious systemic racism, bias or bigotry.

We Begin Our Journey of Understanding

Jasser's book *A Battle Souls Islam*, published in 2013, discusses how Islam should be reformed, and where mainstream Islam is leading North America, and by extension all of Western civilization.

After 9/11, Jasser organized an outdoor demonstration in support of America and against Islamic terrorism. The event was widely publicized and promoted by news outlets. There were eleven local mosques in the immediate vicinity of the demonstration and Jasser invited their Imams to speak. However, no Imams attended, and of about four hundred attendees, most were non-Muslim. (Battle Souls Islam, p.11).

Why did the Imams stonewall Jasser's rally? Those who interviewed him on his book promotion circuit did not seem interested in asking. Perhaps they had not read the book.

Jasser's book received many favorable reviews. Most remarked how refreshing it was to encounter such an eloquent case for the reformation of Islam.

If It Looks Like a Duck... Maybe It Is Not a Duck

Near the beginning of the book (Battle Soul Islam) Dr. Jasser tells us that Islamic scholars, literature and doctrine inform us that Islam in its true nature is violent toward non-believers.

When George Bush and others after 9/11 said, "Islam is a religion of peace," were they mistaken? Or were they misinforming the population for the sake of inter-religious community cohesion? Many, including boxer Mohammad Ali (Battle Soul Islam), were motivated in this effort to suppress rising anti-Islam sentiment. One week after the attack, President Bush gave a speech at a mosque surrounded by members of CAIR. He said nice things about Islam:[8]

> *These acts of violence against innocents violate the fundamental tenets of the Islamic faith. And it's important for my fellow Americans to understand that.*

8 https://youtu.be/liudIJFg8UQ

Dr. Jasser tells us that Islamic doctrines and Muslim scholars are violently opposed to non-Muslims. How then can George Bush say with certainty that the attack on the Twin Towers went against the tenets of Islam? Someone is very misinformed – or deliberately misleading the public for the sake of community cohesion.

Who Is in Conflict with Whom?

Jasser tells us (Battle Soul Islam) "America is not in conflict with my Islam."

America was not in conflict with Japan until they were attacked at Pearl Harbor. Jasser does not say that Islam is not in conflict with America. But he does say that Islamism must be defeated because it is completely at odds with secular values.

Unlike political ideologies, Islam does not manage affairs of the state to achieve political objectives, but for spiritual ones. Allah *MHNBE* has decreed how civil and state matters are intertwined. All that is civic affects what is spiritual and vice versa. Islam has elevated what could be considered mundane state affairs to a higher calling. Take the post of transportation minister. Many will assume transportation is about the movement of people. That is just half of it. The other half is how to manage this so that it complies with Shari'ah and the many added intricacies, such as verifying women's travel authorization slips, and gender separation.

Dr. Jasser tells us "Islamism is completely at odds with secular values." (Battle Soul Islam) History has shown us that two tribes completely at odds with each other will soon be at war. One of these Muslim tribes propagates Islamism:

> *To defeat Islamism is a Muslim reformation. We Muslims must modernize our interpretation of Islam and bring it into harmony with liberty so that the more antiquated aspects of Shari'ah, cutting off hands, killing those that leave Islam, second-class status of women become things of the past. (Battle Soul Islam)*

Dr. Jasser and the reform movement often mention that Islam has not yet gone through a reformation as Christianity has. This statement presupposes that a reformation is going to happen. For argument's sake, let us accept that the Islam reformation is coming. What will be the basis for this reformation? Dr. Jasser might not be aware that Martin Luther in Germany, John Calvin in Switzerland and King Henry VIII in England relied on Christian doctrine to legitimize the Reformation. Islamic doctrine and scholarship do not support the Muslim reform movement. Islamic doctrine contains specific safeguards to ensure Islam will never be reformed.

Reformers have stated on many occasions that cutting off of limbs and stoning to death must stop.

The following are two Hadith that instruct on stoning and amputating:

Ibn al-Qayyim:

> *Those whom the Messenger of Allah PBUH stoned for zina were well known and few in number, and their stories were recorded and are well known. They were the Ghaamidi woman, Maa'iz, the woman who committed adultery with the hired worker, and the two Jews.*

at-Turuq al-Hukmiyyah:

> *With regard to amputations, the Prophet PBUH cut off the hand of a male thief and a female thief.*
>
> *Al-Bukhaari (6788) and Muslim (1688) narrated from 'Aa'ishah (may Allah be pleased with her) that the Quraysh were concerned about the case of the woman who had stolen, then he ordered that the hand of that woman who had stolen be cut off.*

Some people – Dr. Jasser included – contend that there is an element of the Muslim community that promotes the supremacy of Muslims and Islam (Battle Souls Islam, p.39). This is in keeping with what several senior Imams in the West – Yasir Qadhi, Abu Ameenah Bilal Philips, Karim AbuZaid, Raj Wahadj, Mustafa Farooq (CEO of NCCM) and Younus Kathrada – say about non-Muslims living under dhimmitude (humiliated) status.

How can we resolve the stark differences between Shari'ah, Muslim Arabic culture, LGBTQ+ and women's rights within the framework of democracy? Dr. Jasser tells us it cannot be done (Battle Souls Islam, p.114): "This conflict will not be resolved with elections." Dr. Jasser also tells us that "fixing" Islam will take "generations" (Battle Souls Islam, p.39) and will require "institutional investment." Will it take twenty, forty or one hundred generations? Institutional investment usually refers to hospitals, bridges, electric grids, pipe lines, and tunnels.

CHAPTER 5

HOW FAR IS THE REACH OF "BAD" ISLAM?

In this chapter we will try to understand the extent to which the misunderstood Islam (Islam associated with violent jihad) has penetrated a foundational American institution.

Major Nidal Hasan is Shooting

In 2009, Major Nidal Hasan killed thirteen and wounded thirty unarmed American soldiers at the Fort Hood Army base. President Obama's first official act following the attack was to make certain that the image of Islam was not besmirched. He said, "This is not an Islamic attack, but workplace violence." Whenever there is an attack by a person identifying as a Muslim, officials quickly conclude that it was not an act related to Islam but rather a mental health issue.

However, US Navy Lieutenant Dr. Jasser disagrees with President Obama's assessment. He wrote that this was a militant Islamist terrorist act committed because of Nidal Hasan's affiliation with radical homegrown American jihadist, Imam Anwar al-Awlaki (Battle Souls Islam, p.149). Imam al-Awlaki was President of the Colorado University Muslim Students Association. After his graduation in 1994, he became an Imam at the Denver Islamic Society and then from 1996-2000 in a San Diego mosque. After 9/11, he advised the FBI on counter-terrorism measures. He was interviewed by *Time* magazine and invited to speak at the White House. Prior to 9/11, several high-profile American jihadists were congregants at al-Awlaki's mosque, including Major Nidal Hasan. Imam al-Awlaki continues to influence Muslims in America.

American Intelligence eventually caught on to the fact that al-Awlaki was a high-level jihadist operative, not far different from Osama bin-Laden. A few years after the attack at Fort Hood, President Obama approved a targeted drone strike that killed al-Awlaki in Yemen during the "War on Terror." At the time, this was seen as controversial because al-Awlaki, unlike bin-Laden, was an American citizen who was killed without the benefit of due process afforded under the American Constitution.

Before going on his killing spree, Dr. Hasan, an army psychiatrist, addressed a small group of medical officers, explaining what motivates other Muslims in the American army to kill their fellow American soldiers.

The following is a partial transcript of a talk Major Hasan gave not long before his shooting spree:

> *It represents my research and again, the Quranic worldview as it relates to Muslims in the US Military. The reason I chose Quranic worldview as opposed to Muslim worldview is because*

sometimes there can be a huge disconnect between what the Quran teaches and what Muslims actually do. And that disconnect can sometimes be explained by cultural interactions between culture and political factors, which I am not going to get into because it can get quite confusing.

So, the objective: I hope the audience will be able to identify what the Quran inculcates in the minds of Muslims and the potential implications that may have for the US Military… One particularly infamous case was Hasan Akbar, who threw a couple grenades into fellow soldiers' tents, killing and injuring several. So I think it's important from that respect.

Also, I hope to describe the nature of the religious conflicts that Muslims may have with the current wars in Iraq and Afghanistan…

The consensus is that Islam is the peace one attains when one fully submits to God… An Islamist is one who advocates rule by God's law.

Then, the concept of jihad, it really spans a spectrum. We talked about the lesser jihad, and what we mean by that is the actual fighting part of jihad. So, sometimes that's associated with holy war. It doesn't have to be, but it can be…

Muslims in the armed forces. Qaseem Uqdah, who actually was the head of the American Muslims Armed Forces and Veterans' Affairs Council in Washington DC, counted upward [of] 15,000 and if you ask some of the chaplains, they probably agree [with] that number, at least in 2001. [In] the military, the largest group of Muslims would be the African-Americans, followed by Indo-Pakistanis, Arabs and then Caucasians…

American Imams have said that you can be in the military as long as you're following Quranic injunctions...

A Muslim soldier said, "It's getting harder and harder for Muslims in the service to morally justify being in the military that seems constantly engaged against fellow Muslims." And here are verses that are of interest. 4.93: "...and whosoever kills a believer intentionally, his punishment is hell he shall abide in it, and Allah will send his wrath on him and curse him and prepare for him a painful chastisement."

Clint Watts is a fellow at the Foreign Policy Research Institute and a national security contributor for NBC News and MSNBC. In an extensive report, he concluded that there were three contributing factors to Major Hasan's radicalization:

1) *He harboured divided loyalties.*
2) *The death of his mother pushed him to become religious.*
3) *He gravitated to the conservative mainstream Islam preached at the Dar al-Hijrah mosque in Falls Church, Virginia. The mosque was attended by two of the 9/11 hijackers.*

Imam Anwar al-Awlaki also preached that the "War on Terror" was a war against all Muslims. Watts concluded that this was what led Major Hasan to kill thirteen soldiers in an Islamic-inspired terror attack.[9]

Are there other mosques and Imams like al-Alwaki in the West that are incubating Muslim jihadists?

---

9 https://www.fpri.org/article/2011/06/major-nidal-hasan-and-the-fort-hood-tragedy-implications-for-the-u-s-armed-forces/

> *There are plenty of radical mosques in [America]. Many mosques preach an Islamism extremism that is non-violent but is a precursor of Islamist extremism that influenced Hasan.* (Battle Souls Islam, p.150)
>
> *Many Islamist groups want to destroy the West as we know it by whatever means necessary and impose their interpretations of Shari'ah.* (Battle Soul Islam)

Dr Jasser is not saying anything that has not been said by both Islamophobes and North American and European Muslim scholars and Islamic organizations. Here we have a case in which "radical" Imams and Islamophobes are in agreement.

Evolution Is to Naturally Evolve

Dr. Jasser tells us that "radicalization is a natural evolution for an individual consumed by the Islamist narrative." (Battle Soul Islam) Islamic doctrine combined with the history of Islam is the Islamist narrative. What Dr. Jasser deems "radical," mainstream Muslims see as sincere, absolute, unquestioning devotion and submission to the will of Allah to bring justice and peace to all humanity.

According to Islamic scholars, there are several documented cases where devout pious Muslims committed acts of terrorism. One such example occurred in Saudi Arabia in 1979; a group of approximately four hundred Muslim students hijacked the Kaaba in Mecca. They held people hostage for fourteen days, killing one to five hundred, until they were subdued by Special Forces from France. What does this and similar incidents say to the Western media and academics that venerate pious Muslims?_

Imam Yasir Qadhi about the pious Muslim who led the attack on the Kaaba:

> *I was reading his documents with a fine-tooth comb. It seemed to be very solid, very well argued, very passionate. And this terrified me that I could find nothing wrong or deviant... Most of the people with him were from the University of Medina.* https://youtu.be/Kj-JkIoOO-Q[10] YouTube 2014

This seems to indicate a possible causal relationship between Muslim religiosity and Islamic terrorism.

> *...**the problem of radicalization among the faithful**... We Muslims are the only ones with the knowledge to reform the root causes of radical Islamism. (*Battle Souls Islam, *p.187)*

This statement presupposes that solving the "root" cause is important. If someone is tapping your head with a hammer, the "root cause" is of little importance. Those standing around watching your head being tapped with a hammer might be interested to know the "root cause." The person tapping your head with the hammer might not be in touch with their inner feelings and motivations that drive them to tap your head with a hammer. But you just want the head-tapping to stop and care nothing about the "root cause."

Dr. Jasser tells us that the homegrown Islamist terrorist threat continues to grow in America. Right-wingers and Islamophobes say the threat is also growing in Europe, Canada, America and Australia.

---

10 https://youtu.be/Kj-JkIoOO-Q

> *As recently foiled plots reveal, Al-Qaeda and other groups still have their own operatives waiting to strike. But we must realize that* ***propaganda can be just as powerful a weapon as a bomb****.* *(*Battle Souls Islam, p.232*)*

Islam promotes the concept of "peace and justice." But what many do not consider is that these concepts can mean different things to different people. When true believing Muslims say "peace," they mean peace as defined by Islam. This peace will come when all of humanity embraces and submits to Islam. Similarly, justice is defined by Shari'ah. When all Muslims and non-Muslims in North America, Australia and Europe, live under the Shari'ah, there will be justice as defined by Islam.

CHAPTER 6

MUSLIMS INFLUENCING SOCIETY

In this chapter we look at the political influence Muslim reformers wield in Canada and how that is aiding the Muslim reform movement. We compare that to the political influence of mainstream Islam that rejects reformers as misguided deviants.

Muslim Lobby in Canadian Government

In his bid to become leader of Canada in 2015, Justin Trudeau relied on the support of the Muslim community and its organizations. One of these organizations was the Canadian Council of Imams (CCI).

According to Jasser (Battle Souls Islam, p.164), the world-renowned Imam Yusuf al-Qaradawi wrote a paper on apostasy that reads like a theocratic supremacist manifesto and was endorsed by Canadian Imam Yusuf Badawi, a senior member of CCI. CCI advises the Canadian federal government and accredits Imams. This indicates that the voice of mainstream Muslims has a great influence in Canada. According to the organization Muslim Vote, Muslims can be a deciding factor in 33% of the electoral seats across Canada.

In 2020, I attended a political BBQ meet-and-greet for a Mr. Moshen, who was running for the PC seat in Scarborough. Mr. Moshen is a member of the Muslim Bangladeshi community and virtually everyone in attendance was from this community. I made a point of engaging several people: "Hi…so tell me, why are you voting for this candidate?"

"He is from my community."

"And why is that good for Canada?"

They would stare at me in silence.

I had this conversation perhaps fifteen times. What became evident was that this group of fine upstanding citizens was not concerned with Canada but with advancing their ethnic community.

> *We need to get a Bangladeshi elected to advance the Bangladeshi people.*

Individual Bangladeshis seem to unite as a tribe. Will their love for Allah motivate them and other Middle Eastern and African tribes/communities to unite under the banner of Islam or an Asian group? If it did, they would dominate politics at all levels. In 2050 or so this diverse group will have a definitive numerical voting advantage throughout Canada. Until 2050 that advantage is only for most large urban centers.

Toronto Imam Jawed Anwar:

> *Politics is a tool for grabbing power and pursuing the interest of a party, person, tribe, class or nation. But for Muslims, it is the Holy jihad for fulfilling Islam's civilizational goal.* [11]

11 https://www.as-seerah.com/Muslims-Betrayal-of-the-Civilizational-Role_397.html

Children Birthing Babies

Politics intersects with interfaith bridge-building pluralism. Toronto Police Muslim Chaplain Musleh Khan, a member of CCI, in 2017 publicly endorsed men fathering children with nine-year-olds. Without contextualization, some will misunderstand what the Imam was actually endorsing. Prophet Mohammad *PBUH* married Aisha when she was six or seven. However, he did not consummate the marriage until she matured at the age of nine. According to Imam Khan, nine-year old girls back then were mature like thirty year-old women are today. Musleh Khan's comments, some say taken out of context, caused controversy for a brief moment. However, he remained in this trusted position.[12]

Supporting Mainstream Islam

The Muslim Lobby is amassing power in all Western governments. Many of these groups represent a constituency that is small in overall numbers, but because of unwavering commitment, organizational abilities and financial resources, they are able to exert disproportionate influence. Those considered Right-wing or Islamophobes say politicians use these groups to get elected. These groups then use politicians to further their agenda.[13] For many politicians, the priority is to remain in or to gain power. The annual salary for an MP in Canada is $157,000, with an additional $75,000 for a cabinet post. After six years of service, the pension plan is most generous.

12 https://youtu.be/NLNcKgO-hCI

13 https://www.huffpost.com/archive/ca/entry/canadian-muslim-vote-eid-dinner-justin-trudeau_ca_5d0e87a2e4b0a39418636a3e

Is it possible a minister will advocate for policies that are not in the interest of the nation but of the group that got them elected?

Islamism Infiltrating Western Governments

Dr. Jasser informs us that Minnesota Attorney General and former US Congressman Keith Ellison is a key member of the American Islamist movement (Battle Souls Islam, p.202). As of 2022, Attorney General Ellison has not demanded a retraction or brought a civil suit against Dr. Jasser.

Skeptics of Muslim reform allege that Islamists have long since infiltrated Canadian politics. They point to the Muslim caucus in the Liberal Party comprised of MPs Omar Alghabra, Ahmed Hussein, Iqra Khalid and others[14] that regularly meet to address issues pertaining to the Muslim community. In contrast, no Muslim reformers have attained political positions in any Western government.

Canadian MP Omar Alghabra:

> *It could have been assumed to malign certain groups including the Muslim community and who just first to draw attention to the government of this mistake NCCM who led this charge, Ihsaan Gardee and his team reaching out to government officials to ministers their staff. I am here to tell you that next week the word Shia, Sunni and Islam will be removed.*

Public Safety Canada amended its 2018 report. This is in line with Justin Trudeau and the Liberal Party's stance on Islamophobia.

14 https://unpublishedottawa.com/letter/306270/liberal-muslim-parliamentary-caucus-deeply-concerned-about-threats-made-downtown

Canada has officially recognized that Islam is a religion of peace, justice and equity. Those who associate Muslim suicide jihadists or terrorists with the religion of Islam are guilty of Islamophobia.

Toronto Imam Syed Rizvi:

> *You have to study the* ***political system*** *of Canada, how it works, and how you can engage with the system for the betterment of the country as well as the minorities,* ***especially for the Muslim minority****. The ultimate purpose should be to promote justice in society for all citizens, especially the minorities... You have to look at minorities around yourself in Canada and you will see almost all of them are religious and ethnic communities ... they're fully engaged with the system in order to* ***safeguard their own interest locally as well as internationally.***[15]

Skeptics argue that reformers are not reforming Islam, but rather mainstream Islam is reforming Canada and the West. The Muslim community's first major victory was in getting the Canadian government to pass M-103. This motion officially recognizes that Islam is a religion of peace and is greatly contributing to Canada and all mankind. Adopting this motion triggered a process that mandates considerable funding be made available for anti-Islamophobia NGOs. A standing committee was set up by the Department of Canadian Heritage, consisting of forty members led by the Hon. Hedy Fry (" [B. C.], where crosses are being burned as we speak").[16] This committee

15 https://youtu.be/AxgVD8EvJAM

16 https://www.cbc.ca/news/canada/fry-says-she-s-sorry-about-cross-burning-allegation-1.295188

undertook a major year-long study and came up with an extensive list of recommendations, including:

1. Recommends updating and reinstating the previous Canadian Action Plan Against Racism and broadening it to include religious discrimination through consultations with civil society, grassroots organizations, and interfaith groups.
2. Recommends the creation of a directorate at the Department of Canadian Heritage that will develop, implement and monitor this National Action Plan.

30. That January 29th be designated a National Day of Remembrance and Action on Islamophobia, and other forms of religious discrimination.

Some argue that these provisions would subvert either directly or inadvertently Western civilization's sacred value of free speech. It would give a governmental regulatory bureaucracy the ability to say what is and what is not permitted.

This brings us to **Bill C-36,** that enables a judge to punish a hate crime that may be committed in the future. The bill aims to:

- amend the Canadian Human Rights Act to define a new discriminatory practice of communicating hate speech online, and to provide individuals with additional remedies to address hate speech;
- add a definition of "hatred" to section 319 of the Criminal Code based on Supreme Court of Canada decisions; and
- create a new peace bond in the Criminal Code designed to prevent hate propaganda offences and hate crimes from being committed.[17]

---

17 https://www.canada.ca/en/canadian-heritage/news/2021/07/the-government-

810. § 012 (1) A person may, with the Attorney General's consent, lay information before a provincial court judge if the person **fears on reasonable grounds** that another person **will commit a hate crime.**

(8) ***The Commission*** *may deal with a complaint in relation to a discriminatory practice described in section 13* ***without disclosing*** to the person against whom the complaint was filed or to any other person, ***the identity of the alleged victim,*** *the individual or group of individuals who has filed the complaint or any individual who has given evidence or assisted the Commission in any way in dealing with the complaint,* ***if the Commission considers*** that there is a real and substantial risk that any of those individuals will be subjected to threats, intimidation or discrimination.

Those appointed to these commissions have an impressive record as advocates for social justice. Critics point out that most have no experience in the legal profession. Proponents argue that attaining equitable and just outcomes supersedes the concept of evidentiary procedure or a reliance on facts. All commissions have, at a minimum, a 98.6% success rate.

(9) In this section, hate speech means the content of a communication that expresses detestation or vilification of an individual or group of individuals on the basis of a prohibited ground of discrimination.

---

of-canada-concludes-national-summit-on-islamophobia.html

Could Muslim Reformers Be Deemed a Hate Group?

Professor Manji and Dr. Jasser have both made written statements about individual Imams and Islam that could be targeted by these tribunals or law C-36. In Europe, there have been several cases where ex-Muslims were convicted of hate speech.

> *One aspect of Islamism that is less obvious to most Americans is the existence of sophisticated lobby groups committed to supplanting secular law with Shari'ah,* (Battle Souls Islam, p.224).

The above statement could be seen as bringing hate upon Islam or certain Muslim groups. Once a complaint is made, the wheels are set in motion. An investigation in itself can be very inconvenient for the party being investigated with the full force, resources and finances of the state.

M-103 sets the bar or sociological understanding of what is deemed as hate. M-103 states that linking Islam with Muslims who commit terrorism is Islamophobia:

> *Bill C-36:* ***(1. § 1)*** *For greater certainty, the Commission shall, under paragraph (1) § (d), decline to deal* with a complaint filed on the basis of section *13* if it is *plain and obvious* to the Commission *that the complaint indicates no hate speech, as defined in subsection 13(9).*

People who lean to the right point to the language "plain and obvious to the Commission." They argue that the Commission is made up of people who were appointed because they are amenable to the government's policies and therefore are partial toward equity and social justice. They also say that the term "plain and obvious" is a great departure from "reasonable" or "on balance of probabilities." Bill C-36, they argue, operates under the premise of a reverse onus. The prosecution only needs to establish the slight possibility of a potential crime, whereas the defendant must prove with near certainty that no future hate crime will be committed.

> *Islamism has grown more sophisticated. Muslims with Islamist leanings have become quite influential in our government.* (Battle Souls Islam, p.224)

Professor Manji:

> *Instead of acknowledging a serious* ***problem with the guts of this religion,*** *we reflexively romanticize Islam.* (The Trouble with Islam, p.54)
>
> *I began to grasp how Islam came to be an insular,* ***often hateful religion****.* (p.72)

Could someone complain to the Commission that these statements are hateful or could be interpreted as hateful? Yes. An investigation would commence. The Commission could conclude that it is obvious but not "plainly obvious."

> *(3) If the provincial court judge before whom the parties appear is satisfied by the evidence adduced that the informant has reasonable grounds for the fear, the judge may order that the defendant enter into a recognizance to keep the peace and be of good behaviour for a period of not more than 12 months.*
>
> *(6) The provincial court judge may add any reasonable conditions to the recognizance that the judge considers desir-*

able to secure the good conduct of the defendant, including conditions that:

- *(a) require the defendant to wear an electronic monitoring device, if the Attorney General makes that request;*
- *(b) require the defendant to return to and remain at their place of residence at specified times;*
- *(c) require the defendant to abstain from the consumption of drugs, except in accordance with a medical prescription, of alcohol or of any other intoxicating substance;*
- *(d) require the defendant to provide, for the purpose of analysis, a sample of a bodily substance prescribed by regulation on the demand of a peace officer, a probation officer or someone designated under paragraph 810.3(2)(a) to make a demand, at the place and time and on the day specified by the person making the demand, if that person has reasonable grounds to believe that the defendant has breached a condition of the recognizance that requires them to abstain from the consumption of drugs, alcohol or any other intoxicating substance.*

811. A person bound by a recognizance under section 83.3, 810, 810.01, 810.1 or 810.2 who commits a breach of the recognizance is guilty of (a) an indictable offence and liable to imprisonment for a term not exceeding two years; or (b) an offence punishable on summary conviction.

Refusal to enter into recognizance

(5) *The provincial court judge may commit the defendant to prison for a term of not more than 12 months if the defendant fails or refuses to enter into the recognizance.*

Many will applaud this initiative by the Liberal government of Justin Trudeau in the hope that it will quell notorious Islamophobes. Will M-103, Bill C-36 or the Canadian Human Rights Commission be asked to designate the Muslim reform movement a hate group that spreads or encourages hatred of Islam? Skeptics ask not if they will, but why they will not.

According to Dr. Jasser, Muslims are using their increasing resources and political influence to supplant Western values, laws and traditions with those of Islam (Battle Souls Islam, p.204). But is this true? Are the foundational elements that support mainstream Islam being solidified? And if they are, is it at the expense of reform Islam? Others say that asking such questions is irresponsible, incendiary and a preposterous notion undeserving of consideration. Those that advocate for a full and robust answer to the above cite the recent Canadian National Summit on Islamophobia.

Canada Concludes the National Summit on Islamophobia

> The Ministry of Heritage put out a press release on July 22, 2021: [18]

The big news is that the Federal Government in partnership with the Muslim community is pledged to do its utmost to stamp out fear or hate of Islam.

18 *https://www.canada.ca/en/canadian-heritage/news/2021/07/the-government-of-canada-concludes-national-summit-on-islamophobia.html*

- *A renewed focus on dedicated resources to support the work within government to combat Islamophobia and all forms of hate.*
- *The Honourable Diane Lebouthillier, Minister of National Revenue, has requested that the Taxpayers' Ombudsperson conduct a systemic study to address the concerns of Muslim led charitable organizations;* (this is in regards to the Ottawa mosque losing charitable status due to alleged hate speech and financial malfeasance).
- *Take a whole-of-government approach by working with departments across the government to take further action on these priorities.* This will entail a human resources audit of all government institutions, and those doing business with the government. It could take up to ten years and cost billions. Meanwhile, the short- and medium-term funds are immediately available to Muslim organizations.

These are two of the organizations to receive such funding:

- **$199,000 to Al Ihsan Educational Foundation**. PROJECT: Expansion of the online hate project addressing Islamophobia to also include anti-Asian online hate.
- **$349,210 to the Muslim Association of Canada.** PROJECT: Addressing systemic barriers to social participation for Muslim girls, specifically in sports, by providing them with tools and support to improve their representation.

With a cursory look into their online messages, it is apparent that both of these organizations are at odds with the modern liberal progressive Islam promoted by reformers.

Mufti Aansim Rashid is President of Al Ihsan Educational Foundation. This organization, according to its website, adheres to the Islam of the Sahaba (Companions) and Rashidune (Four Rightly Guided Caliphs). They also include an excerpt from blog post #5, "Conquest of Khaibar": [19]

> *Allah has promised you abundant spoils that you will capture, and he has hastened for you this, and he has restrained the hands of men from you: Surah Al fath ... 48 verse 20-21*

The author of the post explains the Islamic definition and benefits of "spoils":

> *The phrase "many spoils" mentioned here refers to the sizable spoils that fell into the hands of Muslims in the conquests which followed the victory at Khaibar, in the rest of Arabia and the neighboring countries. This verse embodies [the] prophecy that Muslims will achieve other great victories after the victory of Khaibar and in consequence many spoils until the end of the world.*

Some argue that acquiring spoils of war -- sometimes referred to as war booty -- was the primary factor in the spread of Islam.

According to the *Saheeh International Quran*, distributed at Toronto's Dundas Square:

> *4:24 And also prohibited to you are all married women except those your right hand possesses.* (152) (i.e. slaves or war captives who had polytheist husbands.)

---

19 https://ihsan.ca/weekly_blog/4-the-sahaba-our-role-models/

48:19 *And much more booty which they will take. And ever is Allah exalted in might and wise.*

When we learn more about war booty, we understand that Muslim reformers will need considerable assistance to quell the lust some Muslims feel is their right and obligation to Allah.

Ruling on Muslims' War Booty

So enjoy what you have gotten of booty in war, lawful and good' ***[al-Anfaal 8:69]****. What is meant here by booty (ghaneemah) is wealth in the form of money, property and other useful things taken from the kuffaar.*

Verily, one-fifth (1/5th) of it is assigned to Allah, and to the Messenger, and to the near relatives [of the Messenger. ***[al-Anfaal 8:41]***

The other four-fifths are to be shared out among the mujaahideen who took part in the fighting, by giving one share to each foot-soldier and three shares to each horseman (one share for him and two for his horse. ***[al-Anfaal 8:41]***

It is worth pointing out that reformist Muslims who support Western values and a modern liberal progressive Islam receive no funding from the Canadian government, while Muslim organizations that promote the traditional conservative Islam that teaches children that "homosexuals are cursed by Allah", restricts women's ability to leave the house, and promotes the concept of war booty receive funding. If Western governments continue to fund mainstream Islam, there will be no Islamic reformation. [20]

---

20 https://ihsan.ca/weekly_blog/4-the-sahaba-our-role-models/

CHAPTER 7

LGBTQ+ AND WOMEN LEARN THEIR ISLAM

In this chapter we explore the rich tapestry that over generations has instructed Muslims on interpersonal relationships.

> *From the beauty of Islam is the great importance and attention it awards to Muslim girls and women. And then follows that there be specific rules and guidance that Muslim women are to adhere to in their daily family lives, social lives, workplace, and more.*
>
> *This course delivers the knowledge Muslim women need in order to follow the Commandments of Allah in their everyday lives.* (p.51 p.88) [21]

The following hadith is considered strong by some Muslim scholars. It is incorporated into the teaching of some madrasas in the West but not all:

21 https://ihsan.ca/muhsinaat/

> *...if a man were covered from head to foot with weeping sores oozing pus, and his wife were to come to him and lick his sores (to clean them), this would not fulfill the rights he has over her.* (Reported by Imaam Ahmad, 12153; Saheeh al-Jaami', 7725)

In April 2017 on the podcast "Let the Quran Speak," a young Muslim woman interviewing Imam Shabbir Ally asked if any Muslims believed or followed the above Hadith. Imam Ally replied that this Hadith is considered authentic and that Muslims are expected to follow it. [22]

The Muslim Association of Canada and Women's Rights

As mentioned, following the 2021 National Summit, The Muslim Association of Canada (MAC) received $349,000 from the Canadian government to address systemic barriers to social participation of girls in sport.

Dr Jamal Badawi is a senior member of MAC. In September 2019, he explained the context of wife-beating in his book *Gender Equity in Islam:*

> *The husband may resort to another measure that may save the marriage, at least in some cases. Such a measure is more accurately described as a gentle tap on the body, but never on the face... As to those women on whose part you fear disloyalty and ill conduct, admonish them [first], [next] refuse to share their beds [and last] beat them (lightly).*[23]

---

22 https://youtu.be/SkTBD2gTV8w

23 ***https://news.acdemocracy.org/canadian-muslim-scholar-explains-the-meaning-of-wife-beating-in-islam/***

Some people, including Muslim reformers, believe that beating women – even if lightly and without leaving marks or breaking bones – goes against human rights and the dignity of the person.

Influenced by Companions of the Prophet

Al Ihsan Educational Foundation states on their site that their role models are the Sahaba (companions of the Prophet). They stress the importance of learning from the Sunnah.[24] The Sunnah and the Sahaba make it clear that apostates, homosexuals, adulterers and blasphemers should be executed, and that marriages are not to be consummated until the female is nine lunar years old (8 1/2 solar years). We learn from the following *saheeh* authentic Hadith, narrated by al-Bukhari:

> *Because it is permissible to marry a young girl does not mean that it is permissible to have intercourse with her. Prophet Mohammad PBUH delayed the consummation of his marriage to 'Aa'ishah. Al-Nawawi said: if the husband and the guardian of the girl agree upon something that will not cause harm to the young girl, then that may be done. If they disagree, then Ahmad and Abu 'Ubayd say that once a girl reaches the age of nine then the marriage may be consummated even without her consent, but that does not apply in the case of a female who is younger. Abu Haneefah said: the marriage may be consummated when the girl is able for intercourse, which varies from one girl to another, so no age limit can be set. This is the correct view. There is nothing in the Hadith of 'Aa'ishah to set an age limit or to*

24 **https://ihsan.ca/weekly_blog/12-the-importance-of-the-sunnah/**

forbid that in the case of a girl who is able for it before the age of nine.

Right-wingers, Islamophobes and those less inclined toward bridge-building interfaith dialogue say men should not have sex with nine-year-old girls. Reformist Muslims support this perspective. They however wield little influence in the mainstream Muslim community. Imam Musleh Khan, Toronto Police Chaplain, said in a lecture that Prophet Mohammad *PBUH* did consummate the marriage with Aisha when she was nine. He did advise that doing so in this society would bring trouble. He made it clear that now is not the time or place to implement this practice. [25]

However, those inclined to build interfaith bridges are far less didactic in their pronouncements of right and wrong. Because making such pronouncements defeats the spirit of respect and tolerance which allows for future interfaith bridge-building dialogue.

Islam and LQBTQ+

According to Wael Shihab, Imam **of the mosque Masjid Toronto, which is officially affiliated with MAC:**

> *Homosexuality is a sinful act in Islam... we should not associate with them and should not take them as friends... In Islam, changing one's sex is not permissible if the person (male or female) has complete male or female sex organs... Given the above, it's my advice for him to return back to his original sex*

25 **https://news.acdemocracy.org/toronto-imam-says-marrying-9-year-old-girl-is-permissible-in-islam-it-has-its-time-and-place/**

> *and go through professional counseling and treatment to lead normal happy life.*[26]

Farrah Marfatia is a Policy and Program Specialist in Schools and Institutions at MAC. She is a former Vice-Principal at Safa and Marwa Islamic School and a former Principal at Maingate Academy in Mississauga, Ontario, located within the Anatolia Islamic Centre. In 2015, she authored a guide entitled *How To Talk to Your Muslim Child*, which provided Muslim parents with advice and tools to cope with topics in the Ontario Ministry of Education's Health Education Curriculum (2015), also known as the sex-ed curriculum.

First an excerpt from Farrah Marfatia's interview with *Toronto Star's* Noor Javed (September 7, 2015):

> *I reached out to guidance counselors and teachers in the public system, and they reviewed [the guide] and gave it their stamp of approval. And then, from a religious perspective, I consulted with three Imams. One of the Imams is also a certified teacher. We had a number of meetings, and they gave me their views from a religious perspective. Overall, about 20 people reviewed it... I am so proud of our community leaders because they have backed it up, and see value in it.*

Islamophobes and Right-wingers ask whose values ?

The first edition of the guide was edited by Sheikh Zahir Bacchus, Sheikh Omar Subedar, Imam Belal Ahmad, B.Ed., OCT, Omar Zia,

---

26 *https://youtu.be/E6GmX0hVS1g*

B.Sc., B.Ed., M.Ed., OCT, Bushra Tobah, Ph.D. (candidate), M.Sc., B.Sc. And Rizwan Wadhera, B.Ed., B.A, OCT.

The guide contains the following, which some Right-wingers and people labeled homophobes will support. Without proper contextualization, it could be deemed as highly discriminatory and hateful:

> *...in terms of homosexuality, it is considered to be a sin in all major monotheistic religions including Islam.* ***The Prophet [Mohammad] told us that homosexuals are cursed by Allah*** as are the men who imitate or dress up like women. This must be communicated to your child in a way that is age-appropriate, *bearing in mind that the rights of* **homosexuals are protected by law** *just as our rights to freedom of religion are.*[27]

To counter LGBTQ+ discrimination, the Canadian Liberal government led by Justin Trudeau, in August of 2022 committed to a five-year, $100-million plan to support LGBTQ+, two-spirit and intersex communities. The media tells us this demonstrates the government's commitment to fight discrimination. It also reported that 75% of the funding will go to community organizations. Will Muslim community organizations receive some of these funds?

Guide for Grades 7 and 8:

> *In Islam* only a man can marry a woman and only a woman can marry a man – *we are not allowed to marry people of the same*

27 *https://news.acdemocracy.org/toronto-sex-ed-guide-for-muslims-homosexuals-are-cursed-by-allah-lgbtq-not-permissible/*

> *gender. When people engage in same-sex relationships they go against the natural disposition (fitrah) of human beings and are unable to reproduce.*
>
> *Being transgender is not permissible in Islam* because choosing to imitate the opposite sex in movements and speech is not permissible in Islam according to saheeh hadeeths [reliable narrations attributed to Mohammad].

The vast majority of citizens in the West do not support mainstream Islam. If given a clear choice they might prefer to support modern liberal progressive Islam. Islamophobes argue that this choice will never be put to a referendum because mainstream Muslim leaders prefer the status quo.

CHAPTER 8

DOCTRINE COMPARED TO PREFERENCE

In this chapter we look at some foundational elements of Islam that are contained in its doctrine. We then place these beside the ideas of those that want to reform Islam. This helps us appreciate the rich and complex task undertaken by Dr. Zuhdi Jasser, Professor Irshad Manji and others in the reform movement.

Muslims are instructed to believe the Quran is the literal and unalterable Word of God, which has been interpreted, studied and analyzed for the past 1400 years. Reformers want to drastically alter the Muslim communities' understanding of what it means to be a Muslim and a servant of Allah *SWT*. The hope that this will happen only partially lies in what Dr. Zuhdi Jasser tells us he fondly remembers about his Muslim family and what they taught him about Islam. He believes there is still much to preserve.

The following is the preamble of the Muslim Reform Movement Declaration; affirmed on December 4th, 2015, signed by fourteen reformers and journalists. Dr Jasser is a founding member.

We are Muslims who live in the 21st century, that stand for a respectful, merciful and inclusive interpretation of Islam.

Living in the 21st century has no bearing on the essence of Islam because Islam is believed to be the timeless will of God. Is Jasser implying that because Muslim reformers are modern, the "old Islam" no longer applies? Or is he implying that the Islam before the 21th century was not *respectful, merciful and inclusive*?

Reformers tell us they are in a Battle Souls Islam; therefore an Islamic renewal must defeat the ideology of Islamism, or politicized Islam, which seeks to create Islamic states, as well as an Islamic caliphate.

Ex-Navy lieutenant Dr. Jasser tells us there is a form of Islam that wants to overthrow the American government. (Battle Souls Islam, p.153, 224) Many in America disagree that such an Islam exists. They believe instead – as Dr. Jasser and Professor Manji have stated in other contexts – that Islam is in its essence compatible with Western values.

If we look to the following teachings of North American Imams, we attain a more nuanced understanding:

Imam Abdool Hamid, Toronto Masjid, 2012:

> *Ultimately, brothers and sisters, our goal as Muslims should be to transform to move it along. Not just to be satisfied with the situation as we find it and try to fit in somehow. That may be necessary initially. But Islam came to transform the lives of people. That is what it did in the time of the Prophet. Brother and sisters, we do not want to take over for the sake of taking over. Of course to improve the lives of people, changes will have*

to be made. So, it may seem from one perspective that Islam took over, so to speak. [28]

Muslim reformers tell us that they seek to reclaim the progressive spirit with which Islam was born in the 7th century. They want to bring it into the 21st century. As we will discuss below, Muslim reformers also support the Universal Declaration of Human Rights, which was adopted by the United Nations in 1948.

In the same vein, one could say, "We want to reclaim the capitalist free market system that communism was originally created with." When one does this, one is injecting an assertion about communism as though it is a commonly accepted truth. He who makes the extraordinary claim bears a high burden of proof. A claim is not an argument and certainly not proof. Dr. Jasser does the same when he uses the phrase: "...progressive spirit with which Islam was born." [29]

One might wonder why, when Dr. Jasser states this, he is never challenged. There are several reasons for this. First, most who interview Dr. Jasser have little or no knowledge about Islamic doctrine. They simply accept what he says. Second, everyone in the audience likes what he is saying.

Does Islam Support the United Nations Declaration of Human Rights?

The Islamic Word is represented by the OIC, the Organization of Islamic Cooperation, which is a 56-seat Islamic voting bloc in the United Nations. The countries of the OIC are located primarily in

---

28 *https://youtu.be/C9BssU5ajpg*

29 **https://aifdemocracy.org/**

North Africa, the Near East, and South Asia and make up about 24% of the world's population. The Cairo Declaration is the Islamic response to the UNDHR. In it we learn that Muslim reformers are correct in their assertion that Islam supports free speech. For example:

Article 18 of the UNDHR:

> *Everyone has the right to freedom of thought, conscience and religion –*

Article 22 of the Cairo Declaration:

(a) *Everyone shall have the right to express his opinion freely in such manner as would not be contrary to the principles of the Shari'ah.*

(b) *Everyone shall have the right to advocate what is right, and propagate what is good, and warn against what is wrong and evil according to the norms of Shari'ah*

"Everyone" in (b) could refer to any randomly formed group that unites under the banner of Islam.

The Cairo Declaration is not endorsed by Western countries. Nevertheless, it influences, to some extent, the values of mainstream Muslim communities thriving in the West.

Right-wingers and Islamophobes will question if Muslims in the West are loyal to the Western countries in which they live, or to Allah. The answer is given by two mainstream Imams, Abu Ameenah Bilal Philips and Yasir Qadhi:

Sheikh Yasir Qadhi:

> *It is your duty as a Muslim to prevent what is haram. First, you do this with force with your hands, if you have the ability.*

> *Second, if you cannot do this with your hands, you do this with your words. Third, if you cannot do this with your words, you do this by hating it in your heart.* [30]

Sheikh Abu Ameenah Bilal Philips:

> *The translation of the Sunnah was the Quran into living practice. So the Sunnah is a living Sunnah. It represents a way of life. Fundamentally a moral way of life. Islam is a moral message. To implement that message [might require] weapons. So there is jihad. Jihad has a place. But ultimately, the goal of jihad is not the spilling of blood. The goal of jihad is not primarily to take the lands of other people, though it may come as a part of the jihad. People's lands and their property may be taken, but that isn't the goal. It is just [a] consequence of military struggle. The losers have to be dealt with And they are dealt with in accordance with principles Islam has set down.* [31]

The following that contrasts with the above is taken from the website *American Islamic Forum for Democracy*, founded by Dr. Jasser.

> ***We reject*** *interpretations of Islam that call for any* ***violence, social injustice and politicized Islam.*** *Facing the threat of terrorism, intolerance, and social injustice in the name of Islam,* ***we have reflected*** *on how we can* ***transform our communities*** *based on three principles:* ***peace, human rights and secular governance.***

30 *https://youtu.be/OZcBC7I9mTA*

31 *https://youtu.be/LH3UJUPZZDY*

VIOLENCE: Dr. Jasser, a high-ranking officer in the U.S. Navy, was employed in an institution that is capable of serious violence. In what capacity does Dr. Jasser deny the same to Islam? I assume he will say that the Navy is governed by the morals of America and only unleashes violence when absolutely necessary. Islamic leaders do say Islam is governed by the morals of Allah and Muslims believe the morals of Allah are far superior to the morals of America. Will Dr. Jasser tell Muslims their belief is wrong? Would doing so be an act of oppression?

SOCIAL JUSTICE: Muslim lobby groups in the entire Western world are tirelessly and with great dedication advocating for peace and social justice. However, confusion and misunderstandings can arise when conflicting interpretations of peace and justice compete for social acceptance.

Those on the Right say social justice is a dangerous concept because concepts are malleable. They say nations should be governed not by concepts but by laws that are based on a foundation of culture, history and tradition. It is believed that such ideas and statements will impede the advancement of multiculturalism, pluralism, social justice and equity.

POLITICIZED ISLAM: We will learn that Islam means complete and total submission without question, reservation, or doubt.

Dr. Jasser rejects the establishment of a caliphate. But Islamic leaders instruct that it is a sacred duty to establish a caliphate. Any Muslim who advocates against a caliphate is by extension rejecting Shari'ah and fighting against the will of Allah *SWT*.

> *I see no conflict between practice of Islam and our respect and love for the United States Constitution* (Battle Souls Islam, p.15).
>
> *This belief system is not in conflict with* **my** *Islam. (Battle Soul Islam*)
>
> *...it is possible to love the US Constitution and the Quran.* (Battle Soul Islam)

During a Newman Lecture, **Professor Manji:**

> *A reformist Muslim is one that recognizes that there are freedom-loving passages in the Quran that too few Muslims and non-Muslims know about.*

This reminds me of an encounter I had in 2008 with Raheel Raza, the founder of Muslims Facing Tomorrow.[32] Raheel Raza was on a panel with the editor of the Hamilton Ontario daily paper, and Michael Coren. This talk took place in a Hamilton synagogue. The entrance fee was $20. Raheel Raza spoke for 30 minutes, as did the other panelists.

Raheel Raza spoke of Islam being hijacked and misunderstood. When question time was announced, I shot up to the microphone. "You spoke of the loving, compassionate verses in the Quran. I have read the Quran and could not find these verses of love and compassion. Can you tell me where they are?"

She replied, "I am not a scholar, I cannot give you the exact number of the verses."

I replied, "Then tell me approximately where or in what chapter."

---

32 *https://muslimsfacingtomorrow.com/about-us/*

We went back and forth several times. I did say that if someone makes a claim they should be able to substantiate it. Her discomfort was obvious to everyone. She began to stutter. Michael Coren came to her rescue, accusing me of being a bully. He and I went back and forth several times. I certainly was not rude, but I was direct in a manner that few are. On the way back to my seat, a woman slapped me on the ass: "Good job."

The 20-dollar fee included Coke, chips, grapes, carrots, and mingling with the panelists. I approached the Rabbi and apologized. He was not interested in my apology and seemed annoyed at my presence.

Of the 30 or so people, no one was eager to chat with me, especially Raheel Raza. Whenever I came near her, she walked away.

Eventually, when she was getting carrots and grapes, I walked up to her. Keeping a respectful distance, I pulled out my Quran and said in a clear, loud voice, "Raheel Raza, this is a Quran. If you can find any of those loving and compassionate verses, I will fall on my knees and convert to Islam right here, right now."

She started to screech, "Help, this man is harassing me!"

"Everybody hear this; I will convert to Islam in front of all of you. Does Raheel not want a convert to Islam or was she lying about those peace-loving verses?"

Again she started to screech.

Just to be clear, I kept my distance; there was no aggressive posture or physical intimidation. We were not in a lonely, dark alley but in a synagogue eating grapes and chips.

I lingered on, trying to engage in conversation. Things were wrapping up. A man dressed in a suit told me my behavior was inappropriate. He came across as a reasonable person. I asked him if he had read the Quran. He replied he had not. I asked him why he thought that Raheel Raza would not want to prove me wrong and get me to convert to Islam, or at least make her point. He did not know how to answer. His wife, who was standing beside him, did not like this conversation. She sternly said, "We have to leave now." As he walked away, he looked back several times.

Why do I tell you this story? Because by simply citing said verses, Irshad Manji and Raheel Raza could easily help us be certain that there are loving and compassionate verses in the Quran, and by extension, love and compassion in Islam. This would also help to combat Islamophobia. As far as I know, the only time the word "compassion" appears in the Quran is in 24:02.

> *Do not feel compassion when administering the 100 lashes because this might cause you to neglect your duty to Allah.*

Is Leaving Treason?

Soon after the death of the Prophet *PBUH*, several tribes tried to leave Islam and revert to their original customs and religion. The Muslims waged war against them. The following will add contextualization:

Human Rights in Islam, and Common Misconceptions- by Dr. Abdul Rahman al-Sheha, distributed by Toronto Dawa'h at the corner of Yonge and Dundas:

> *We should take the following points into consideration concerning apostates.*
>
> *Shari'ah decrees execution for the person who apostatizes. Islam does not treat rejection of the faith as a personal matter ... This rejection is a seed of rebellion in the society. ... Islam only punishes the apostate himself with the simple, direct and very effective deterrent...*
>
> *Execution of such an apostate is, in reality, a salvation for the rest of the society members from the maliciousness and violence he would spread if left to propagate his disbelief and blasphemy among the other members of the society.* (Battle Souls Islam, p.22)

Muslim reformers prefer the writings of the Ammadiyya Imams, who make the case that the Quran does not explicitly prescribe the death penalty for apostates. However, the Quran does prescribe death for insurrectionists. Leaving Islam can be and usually is interpreted as insurrection or encouraging insurrection. The Ammadiyya Imams point to verse 2:257 of the Quran: "There is no compulsion in religion." This and other conciliatory verses are attributed to the Mecca period. According to the majority of Muslim scholars, these verses are abrogated by the Medina period which is, as Professor Manji will tell us (The Trouble with Islam, p.42) "the nasty side of the Quran and how it informs terrorism" Oddly, the revered Imam and scholar of the Ammadiyya, **B.A. Rafiq**, cites the following: [33]

---

33 https://ahmadiyya.ng/believes-that-there-is-no-punishment-for-apostasy

1. *And he who turns back on his heels shall not harm Allah at all. And Allah will certainly reward the grateful.* ***(3:145)***
2. *And whosoever takes disbelief in exchange for belief has undoubtedly gone astray from the right path.* ***(2:109)***
3. *Many of the people of the Book wish out of sheer envy from their own selves that, after you have believed, they could turn you again into disbelievers after the truth has become manifest to them. But forgive and turn away from them, till Allah brings about His decree. Surely, Allah has the power to do all that He wills.* ***(2:110)***
4. *And whoso seeks a religion other than Islam, it shall not be accepted from him, and in the life to come he shall be among the losers.* ***(3:86)***

It is important to note that the Ammadiyya are utterly reviled by mainstream Islam and considered blasphemers of the worst kind. This is because they state that their founder, Ghulam Ahmad, was the final prophet after Mohammad. The Ammadiyya have influence over, at most, 1% of the world's Muslims. Some say this makes them irrelevant.

> *The evidence that the apostate is to be executed is found in the words of the Prophet PBUH: "Whoever changes his religion, execute him."* (Narrated by al-Bukhaari, 2794) [al-Nisa' 4:59]

Making Shari'ah a Reality

September 2018, Osgood Hall held a symposium entitled ISIS – Violence and Deradicalization.

Professor Katherine Bullock:

If we get rid of ISIS there will be another ISIS. The real dilemma is the issue of self-determination versus a European, Western hegemony. The ***majority of the people*** *in the region* ***want an Islamic-informed democratic state*** *... So let's turn to Canada; again there is this culturalist approach, even the word "radicalization" is wrong. It's a problem because radicalization is being defined through this culturalist approach. [Canada and the UK] define a radical as someone who desires to install a caliphate, someone who wants to impose Orthodox Shari'ah. But* ***from an Islamic point of view****, there is absolutely nothing radical about wanting a caliphate or wanting Shari'ah. These are completely normal traditional points of view.*[34]

We learn from Professor Bullock that labelling Muslims who want to impose Shari'ah and carve out an Islamic mini-state as radicals is inaccurate and possibly prejudicial.

Sheikh Abu Ameenah Bilal Philips:

Shari'ah is the law of God, the law of Allah, which is good for all times, all people in all places. That is the reality. Wherever Muslims are able to apply it, it is their duty to apply it, not to force it upon people as a minority in a country of non-Muslims.[35]

We learn that, according to Sheikh Bilal Philips, while Muslims are a minority, they should not attempt to impose Shari'ah law.

In fact, both mainstream Muslims and Islamists have the same goal vis-à-vis the establishing of a caliphate. The following was said

34 https://vimeo.com/133654824

35 https://youtu.be/K-91RRLwEhQ

by an Imam at the conference Darkness of Democracy to Light of Islam, held by Hizb ut-Tahrir in 2016 at Glendale Heights, Illinois:[36]

Islam is not here to integrate; Islam is here to dominate. There is no room for compromise.

Is there a contradiction when one Imam says "there is no room for compromise" and another Imam says they will "not force it upon people [when] a minority in a country of non-Muslims"?

We learn more from highly venerated, Imam Jawed Anawar, who has written hundreds of articles, columns… in English and Urdu. His articles on Islamic Education System, "Intellectual History and Madrasah System in South Asia" got wide recognition. [37]

Toronto Imam Jawed Anwar:

> *The early Muslims are known for military victories against the World Powers, political battles, cultural revolution, educational expansion and huge state-building. Islam's mission and vision – as revealed in the Holy Qur'an and taught by the Prophet PBUH were expressed through their deeds. They raised Islam not only as a religion of obligatory rituals but also as a formidable civilizational force.*

Muslim reformers insist that Islam is a religion that encompasses human rights, free speech and separation of religion and state. Imam Jawed Anwar tells us Islam is committed to military colonization including cultural and religious annihilation. Of course one of these voices is incorrect.

---

36 https://youtu.be/LozOm_Vywa0

37 https://news.acdemocracy.org/the-official-bio-of-jawed-anwar-the-founder-of-the-islamic-party-of-ontario/

CHAPTER 9

FURNITURE BREAKING IN YOUR LIVING ROOM

In this chapter we attempt to understand how misunderstanding Muslims feed the narrative of fear and suspicion and how this transitions into effects, implications and costs on individuals and society.

Could what Dr. Jasser and Professor Irshad Manji tell us about Islam be true? It could. However, those that lead Muslim organizations, give fatwa, hold advanced degrees and teach at prestigious Islamic universities are emphatically at odds with Dr. Jasser and Professor Manji's interpretation of Islam and what it means to be a pious upstanding Muslim.

For most non-Muslims, knowing there are Muslims who support freedom of expression, democracy, Western values and LGBTQ+ rights is a comforting thought.

Many supporters of the Muslim reform movement want to know when the preferred reformed Islam will dominate the mainstream.

Will it happen sooner rather than later? Does it depend on the size of the community that adheres to traditional Islam? We know the reformers are the minority. Many want to know if this minority is growing or shrinking, and at what pace? Who has better operational capabilities?

Do Misunderstanding Muslims Support Violence to Defend Islam?

In 2016, a Pew research poll reported the following figures: [38]

Often Support Terrorism
French Muslims 16%
Spanish Muslims 16%
British Muslims 15%
German Muslims 7%

Rarely Support Terrorism
French Muslims 19%
Spanish Muslims 9%
British Muslims 9%
German Muslims 6%

On average 13% of Muslims in Europe are prepared to sacrifice life in this world for the cause of Allah *MHNBE*. Some will use a car in a Christmas market, on a bridge, blow up an airport, church or train. However, an average of 87% of Muslims do not support, or rarely support, violent jihad.

38 https://www.pewresearch.org/search/suicide+bombing+support

This poll raises several questions. What should be the acceptable number of jihadists living in the West? Should it be based on a percentage or absolute numbers? If the Muslims population increased but the percentage of jihadists remained stable would that be acceptable? Should those who support jihad but don't commit it themselves be considered jihadists?

Others ask if the terms radical, extreme, terrorist or jihadist should be limited to Muslims who are prepared to kill and die for the cause of Allah *SWT*. They use the example of a Muslim father who psychologically molds his daughter so that at the age of five she willingly wears the hijab and the full burqa at the age of twelve, with the understanding that exposing any part of her is sexual provocation akin to prostitution. Or he teaches his sons from infancy that to die and kill for Islam, to become a shaheed, is a man's greatest achievement. Or he could teach his children that Jews are apes and pigs who deserve to be slaughtered, or that musical instruments and church bells are the call of Satan. https://www.ericbrazau.com/islams-war-on-christians-imam-church-bells-are-satanic-prophet-obliterated-the-cross/ Is this man a radical?

What if he makes it known to his children that he does not approve of blowing up buses, trains and planes as a tactic to bring about the fall of Western governments, but at the same time glorifies those who do? How would he or his children be ranked on the extremist scale?

Dr. Jasser answers the question about the father referred to above:

> *[Muslim] children learn from an early age that their country [America] is here to serve them and their religion... For the Is-*

> *lamist there is no such thing as a fellow American unless that fellow American offers a pathway to the Islamization of America.* (Battle Souls Islam, p.41)

In June of 2022, **Mufti Usama Abdulghani**, an Islamic scholar based in Dearborn, Michigan, said in a lecture delivered to the children at the Hadi Institute Youth Community Center:

> *Islam teaches us that Islam is supreme. Not that we want a seat at the table, not that our whole hope is to stop Islamophobia so that we can just be treated like human beings. No, Islam is supreme.* [39]

It can reasonably be argued that, even though this teaching does not advocate violence, nevertheless, it conflicts with interfaith community bridge-building cohesion that is focused on embracing equity and inclusion.

Acceptance Is Good; Embracing Is Better

Islam is a religion that is often understood to be misunderstood. However, if it were understood, that would not alter the perception of those who are perceived to be misunderstanding.

- 23 people murdered and 1017 injured or maimed leaving the Ariana Grande concert in 2017
- 13 people killed and 30 injured at the Fort Hood Army base by Army Major Nidal Hasan in 2009

39 https://www.ericbrazau.com/muslim-children-supremacist-ideology/

- 546 shot,130 killed, 100 critically wounded in Paris at the Bataclan and other places by Muslim asylum seekers in 2015
- 202 killed and 200 wounded in the Bali nightclub bombing of 2002
- 193 killed and 2,050 injured in the Madrid train bombing of 2004
- 8 killed and 48 injured on London Bridge in 2017
- 52 killed and 784 injured on the London Underground and busses in 2005
- 3 killed and 264 wounded in the Boston Marathon bombing in 2013
- 17 killed during the Charlie Hebdo attacks in 2015
- 164 killed and 30 injured in the Mumbai Hotel attack in 2008
- 67 killed and 175 injured in a shopping mall in Kenya in 2013
- 47 killed and 126 injured when two churches in Egypt were blown up on Palm Sunday 2017,
- 269 killed and 500 injured when three churches in Sri Lanka blown up on Easter Sunday 2019
- 86 people killed and 400 injured by a man driving a truck through a crowd celebrating Bastille Day in Nice in 2016
- 12 killed by a man driving a truck through a Christmas market in Berlin, in 2021

Many will also agree that the beheadings of soldier Lee Rigby in London, teacher Samuel Paty in France, two Swedish girls vacationing in Morocco, 86-year-old priest Jacques Hamel in Normandy, 60-year-old priest Olivier Maire, and a woman outside Notre Dame Church in Nice, France were committed by Muslims who misunderstand the religion of Islam.

We can for the sake of interfaith bridge building accept and embrace the idea that Muslim jihadists are misunderstanding. But, however misunderstanding they may be, Muslim jihadists will still do what it is they do. In the meantime, the Muslim reform movement is doing its best to reform Islam.

Language Shapes Understanding

Some Islamic leaders tell us that jihadist attacks are perpetrated by Muslims that misunderstand the true Islam. Muslim organizations and politicians tell us that because Islam is a religion of peace, those perpetrating terror in the name of Islam are by definition not Muslim; furthermore, anyone linking these men to Islam is engaging in Islamophobia and irrational thinking.

The following quotes help us understand the contextualized separation between pious Muslims and misunderstanding Muslims:

Imam Yasir Qadhi:

> *They thought these people [are] righteous people, there's a fine line between fanaticism and righteousness. And that line is sometimes difficult to distinguish, even for people of great knowledge and great stature.*

This coincides with what many Muslim families say about their sons who "radicalize." They report their son was not initially religious but when he started attending the mosque regularly, he grew his beard, changed his clothes, and started praying five times a day.

It seems that for secular Muslims, the gateway to radicalization is the mosque. This brings us back to Dr. Jasser, who says, "Plenty of mosques in America foment home-grown jihadists." (Battle Souls Islam, p.149)

Imam Shabbir Ally:

> *Muslims who will say – once we are talking about the Islamic rule – we are talking about establishing the laws of the Quran and the way of the Prophet Mohammad. On the ground that must be good in and of itself, and I think no Muslim can deny that.* [40]

How Much to Fund Islamic Organizations?

In the West we embrace the idea that Muslim jihadists are misunderstanding Islam. And we should all be sensitive to the sensibilities of the Muslim community and not overreact. The next time Muslims, or those identifying as Muslim, commit terror in the name of Islam, it could be used as a moment in time to learning how they are misunderstanding Islam or the teaching of the Imams and scholars. Only when we learn, can we begin to understand.

However, not all Imams denounce the actions of these "misunderstanding" Muslims. Some senior influential Imams in North America tell us that these Muslims were acting in accordance with the Islamic doctrine. The beheading of the French teacher Samuel Paty is one such instance; Imam Yasir Qadhi told us the beheading was a result of insensitivity to Muslim sensibilities, colonization and Islamophobia.

---

40 https://youtu.be/GGSqnrXqbmM

Toronto Imam Jawed Anwar:

> *Some young blood will make a score. The authorities will hang them but for the Muslim community they are heroes.*[41]

Vancouver Imam Younus Kathrada called the beheaded teacher a "filthy human being" for showing cartoon depictions of Prophet Mohammad *PBUH*. Colorado Imam Karim AbuZaid said the beheading was wrong but that Muslims love the Prophet. "I am sorry, we cannot help it… Why should we be prevented from showing our love for the Prophet?" [42]

Toronto Imam Jawed Anwar:

> *Muslims have the right and responsibility to get revenge for dishonouring the prophets of God, particularly the last Messenger Muhammad.... It is sad to note that instead of criticizing and condemning Samuel Paty for his stupidity, cruelty, and blasphemy, the world, including liberal Muslim scholars, is condemning Ghazi Abdullah Sheeshan Shaheed (shaheed in an honourific)* [43]

The catch is that as more misunderstanding Muslims commit terror, more funding is allocated to fight the Islamophobia, or that is fueled by the Muslim terror attacks. Most if not all of this money, goes to Islamic organizations.

---

41 https://www.as-seerah.com/Blasphemy-of-the-Prophet-Right-to-Revenge-1_308.html

42 https://youtu.be/DXL2X_sxTUo

43 https://www.as-seerah.com/Ghazi-Abdullah-Anzorov-Sheeshan-Shaheed-(R.-A.)_385.html

Prime Minister Justin Trudeau: Speaking about returning ISIS fighters

> *We know that actually someone who has engaged and turned away from that hateful ideology can be an extraordinarily powerful voice for preventing radicalization in future generations and younger people within the community.* [44]

Will Justin Trudeau incrementally or dramatically increase the funding to Muslim organizations in an attempt to solve the "radical" Islamization problem that Dr. Jasser tells us "will take much investment and many generations?" (Battle Souls Islam, p.114)

Muslim Children Are Future Leaders of the West

On July 27, 2022, a video[45] posted to the IslamicTV YouTube channel featuring Shiite children in Houston, TX. The male leading the song is about nineteen years old. On average the children seem to be about ten years old. The following are the words being enthusiastically sung:

> *In spite of my age, I will be your army's commander... May my father and mother be sacrificed for you, I will sacrifice everything for you... I make an oath to be your martyr, Ali. A very long time has passed, every nation is full of tears, don't worry about it, oh my Allah, your soldiers are here without fear.*

These children are pledging their allegiance to the Iranian spiritual leader. The Iranian Ayatollah is for Muslims the equivalent

44 https://www.dailywire.com/news/justin-trudeau-returning-isis-fighters-theyll-be-emily-zanotti

45 https://youtu.be/qxYhO8bqC2c

of the Pope for Catholics. This is a contrast to the Sunni Muslims, who are led by an association of councils.

While Prime Minister Justin Trudeau increases funding to Islamic organizations and welcomes returning ISIS fighters as a powerful voice for deradicalization,[46] Dr. Jasser, Professor Manji and Muslim reformers are waiting for more investment and future generations to "modernize" Islam. The mainstream Muslim community also has plans for future generations. It has identified charter schools as the best way to instill Islamic values into children.

Every Mosque is a School

Toronto Imam Jawed Anwar:

> *Masjid Danforth/Donland is extended to grade 8. It is now a K-8 school. It was not a long time ago; it was 2012, I was sitting in the Masjid office talking with the President and some other board members. We were discussing and convincing how and why every Masjid should have their school.*[47]

The **Green Dome Community Center** in Calgary, Alberta in its first phase (2022) is building a seventy-thousand-square-foot complex that houses a charter school with a cafeteria, gymnasium and auditorium. The cost is estimated to be 15-18 million. This school will be accredited to teach k to 12. The second phase involves building a mosque.

---

46 https://freebeacon.com/national-security/trudeau-isis-fighters-returning-canada-can-powerful-voice-preventing-radicalization/

47 https://www.as-seerah.com/Madinah-Islamic-School-%C2%A0A-School-that-you-can-establish-in-every-Masjid_359.html

The Green Dome community website [48] mission statement declares:

> *The Green Dome will be the best Canadian Islamic school in Alberta where future Canadian leaders are developed.*

The following quotes are from the Muslim youth fundraising appeal for the Green Dome:[49]

Talha Amin:

> *Your kids can learn math, chemistry, physics, anything they want. But they should learn those things in an environment that promotes Islam.*

Some ask if, before the City of Calgary issued the building permit, they should have ascertained what Islam will be promoted at this school. Will it be the modern, progressive LGBTQ+ embracing Islam promoted by Muslim reformers or mainstream fundamental Islam?

Wali Hameed:

> *We request that you donate to our project because currently there are thousands of Muslims in Calgary and not enough schools in the community. It's the need for our community and for future generations. It's the need for our kids.*

Some will say that this constant referral to "our" is a call to tribalism and otherizing.

---

48 https://amcia.org/

49 https://youtu.be/iQAXVdOgHdw?t=223

Zubair Tariq:

The Green Dome Islamic School is run by Almadina. I support the building of Green Dome Islamic School because I feel a connection towards it and not just a connection in terms of religion but because it's a place where I can go and understand concepts that I will not be able to find in [other] school[s]. (https://www.youtube.com/@YasirQadhi)

What if these concepts, taught in Muslim schools, contrast with Canadian or Western values? Would this be accepted and embraced as cultural enrichment through diversity?

Umar Rehan:

The Green Dome Islamic School will not only teach the regular Canadian curriculum, but it will also teach Islamic knowledge, what it means to be a Muslim and how you should live as a Muslim.

What exactly does Umar Rehan mean when he says living as a Muslim? Does it mean as the first 4 rightly guided Caliphs or implementing the pact of Umar or execution for apostates and those who insult Prophet Mohammad PBUH, or that a wife is mandated to provide sex on demand or that Muslim women need permission to leave the house?

Usman Ahmed:

Green Dome Islamic School is going to unite the Muslims of Calgary.

Will this uniting lead to tribalism?

The following quotes are from senior Imams affiliated with CCI, which is in turn is affiliated with the Muslim Council of Calgary. The chairman of MCC, Sheikh Jamal Hammoud, serves as the representative in Canada of the Grand Mufti of Lebanon and the Supreme Muslim Court of Lebanon. The quotes are taken from statements or interviews following the beheading of the French teacher Samuel Paty. These Imams influence the organizations mentioned that in turn influence Muslim charter schools' curriculum in Canada.

Tarik Ramadan was Professor of Contemporary Islamic Studies at Oxford University and a visiting Professor at the Faculty of Islamic Studies (Qatar) and the University of Malaysia Perlis.

> *I think if you look [at what is] happening [in France right now] it's not new. It's a very long process. It started a long time ago. Yasir Qadhi is quite right when he's writing that to understand what is happening to France right now you have to go to the colonization time. It started with the cartoons with Charlie Hebdo and all the murders. What is happening is the far right party is taking advantage. In fact, they may lose the election but they are winning as to the discourse. Now we have the normalization of the far right discourse about Islam and Muslims in the name of Laïcité and the secularists system and they are instrumentalizing these attacks [publicly displaying cartoons of Prophet Mohammad PBUH] and everything.* **https://www.youtube.com/embed/uMGS8nLRu0U**

Shaikh Yasir Qadhi:

> *When fascist and far-right xenophobes get power, they foment racism and xenophobia… Secularism can be as terroristic as any religion… [As to the] unfortunate incident of [the] beheading of one teacher, [France] are using that against our nabi [Prophet]… But we cannot ignore provocation. We have to acknowledge that we do have two sets of principles depending on our context. There is a Mecca phase and a Medina phase. … The famous verse of the sword… We understand that in minority situations we do not enact vigilante justice. Harms that will come are far more than any potential good or benefit that you think is going to happen. Are there dissenting voices? Of course … Ibn Taymiyyah –*

NOTE: Muhammad Ibn Taymiyyah, born 1263, Harran, Mesopotamia—died September 26, 1328, Damascus, Syria, one of Islam's most forceful theologians, who, as a member of the Ḥanbalī school founded by Aḥmad ibn Ḥanbal, sought the return of the Islamic religion to its sources: the Qurʾān and the Sunnah, revealed writing and the prophetic tradition. He is also the source of the Wahhābiyyah, a mid-18th-century traditionalist movement of Islam. (https://www.britannica.com/biography/Ibn-Taymiyyah)

> *I mentioned this – you weigh the pros and the cons. … They are using that incident of the beheading of one teacher for doing something to cause this entire campaign against our nabi. This is not about freedom of speech; not at all. Freedom of speech applies when the minority speaks to the majority. One act of millions of Muslims. And one thing these are statistics of any*

crime, any mafia, any negative [event] that happens in the community. But what is the response? Criminalization of the entire religion of Islam. France, who are you to lecture us about the freedom? Who are you to tell us about the crime of one man? This crime that occurred, the teacher that was killed, had nothing to do with the books of fiqh [Islamic law] *and it had everything to do with how you treat your Muslim community. I am not justifying. I am contextualizing. (https://www.youtube.com/@YasirQadhi)*

Imam Dr. Omar Suleiman, CEO Yaqeen Institute, America:

Genocides are carried out in the name of assimilation. It is not Islam that is the problem, it is France… In France the Prophet is portrayed, insulted in the worst of ways. (https://www.youtube.com/watch?v=318q9Zn9LLg)

Sheikh Karim AbuZaid: Colorado, America:

…but Islam is spreading like fire spreads in a dry wood. [Macron's] own people are accepting Islam. One out of ten in France are Muslim. 1.8 billion Muslims, that's the crisis that Emmanuel is feeling. You're afraid because they say in less than 50 years, in the year 2050, Islam will pass Christianity. Someone is insulting the Prophet Mohammad, depicting him in cartoons, the whole Ummah is rising, is saying we can't take it anymore... This love is instilled in our hearts – I have no control over it, I'm sorry ... So why are we blamed for showing this love? … We ask Allah to protect the Muslims, to protect this religion, to protect those who stand for this religion at this time. (https://www.youtube.com/watch?v=T_0GECTMiWE)

Imam Rizvi: Toronto, Canada:

> *The recent events in France and the reaction of President Macron to them is a matter of concern for us… We have previously seen anti-Muslim sentiments in France… expression has its own limitations, especially when it ends up creating hatred towards a visible minority.*[50]

Why did the beheading happen? Who allowed it to happen? Who is responsible? These questions are a worthwhile intellectual exercise that will yield some benefit. But the pertinent questions are: Where is this leading? How does it end? Does it end?

Of course, it goes without saying that these questions will not be entertained by politicians or professors of interfaith bridge-building dialogue (IFBBD) studies. Such questions could be seen to impede the cultural enrichment that diversity brings.

According to Dr. Jasser (Battle Souls Islam, p.204), it is not difficult for Muslim extremists to sell themselves as moderates. The laws that seem to be curtailing free speech also seem reasonable and moderate. But the problem with moderates is that they may only be considered moderate when compared to extreme. Many say that is why we should do away with labels such as "good"/"bad"/"moderate"/"extreme." We must accept and appreciate Islam as it is. There are countless examples of Imams, scholars and world leaders saying "there is no moderate or extreme Islam. There is only Islam." Perhaps it is time we start believing them. If we do this, perhaps we would have a better understanding of Islam and where it is leading us.

50 *https://learningislam.ca/france-crisis/ taken from: https://www.youtube.com/watch?v=GDjbVlmGHGg*

CHAPTER 10

IRSHAD MANJI, REFORMER EXTRAORDINAIRE

In the following chapters, we will look more closely at the implications of Irshad Manji's attempted reformation of the mainstream Muslim community, as well as on non-Muslims living in the West. We do this in three parts:

1. We look closely at what Professor Manji said in an interview as part of the Newman Lectures.
2. We closely examine the book *The Trouble with Islam.*
3. We closely examine the book *Allah, Liberty and Love.*

It is difficult to overestimate the importance of Irshad Manji's leadership in the Islamic reform movement. Her book *Allah, Liberty and Love* is a manifesto for the Muslim Reform movement. The importance of this book can be judged by the reception it received by both mainstream Muslims and the interfaith bridge-building community.

The non-Muslim community warmly and enthusiastically embraces the messages that Professor Manji promotes. The mainstream Muslim community for the most part, if not the complete part, rejects her message, as well as her. There are several reasons for this, but I will touch on just two.

Manji identifies as a lesbian. Mainstream Islam punishes homosexuality with death. But possibly her greater affront to Islam is proposing to reform it. Muslim leaders state that Islam cannot be reformed because it is perfect. To imply it is not perfect is to imply that Islam or the Prophet Mohammad *PBUH* are not perfect. To do this is to commit blasphemy. Professor Manji commits blasphemy on the world stage.

During the Q&A after a screening of Manji's film *Faith without Fear,* a Muslim male commented:

> *To do itjihad you have to be a qualified scholar. If every unqualified Muslim took up itjihad to make rulings on this religion, that would be chaos.*

Professor Manji:

> *I acknowledge in all honesty that what I propose entails the risk of a free-for-all in which anybody can interpret the Quran in any way he or she sees fit. ... I say open up the doors, let a hundred – let a thousand flowers bloom and let's see in the grand marketplace of ideas, whose interpretation suits an emerging generation of Muslims.*

The reference to the blooming flowers comes from Chairman Mao tse Tung. In her answer, Professor Manji inadvertently reveals her level of appreciation for Western Civilization:

Has Professor Manji considered that the marketplace of Muslim ideas in North American universities is dictated by Muslim Student Associations? They, in no uncertain terms, reject reforming Islam and aggressively promote a mainstream fundamental Islam, in line with the Muslim Brotherhood, the Islam that is in Egypt, Afghanistan, Yemen, Chechnya and Pakistan. Should this Islam be given an opportunity to flourish in the West? Many non-Muslims and some Muslims agree it should not. Apparently Irshad Manji is open to this Islam if "in the marketplace of ideas" it is what "suits an emerging generation."

The Newman Lecture

The Newman Lectures are a legacy of St. John Henry Newman (1801-1890), an Anglican priest, scholar and poet who converted to Catholicism and became an important Cardinal. He was canonized in 2019.

On its website, Divine Mercy University tells us that these lectures seek to promote an international conversation among various disciplines. Each lecture is published with an eye toward building a body of learned discussion that is Catholic, both in its breadth of research and in its dialogue with contemporary Catholic-Christian thought.

Bret Stephens interviewed Irshad Manji for this episode. He is an American conservative journalist, editor, and columnist. He began working as an opinion columnist for *The New York Times* and as a senior contributor to *NBC News* in 2017.

Bret Stephens: *What is the calling of a reformist Muslim?*

Manji replied that a Muslim Reformer is a Muslim who has special insight into Islam. They gain this special, somewhat exclusive insight because they recognize that the Quran contains verses about love and freedom that other Muslims do not see.

Professor Manji tells the audience that Reform Muslims should point out these verses, not to embarrass or show up the Muslim unaware of the loving versus, but to illustrate that they do not have the full truth. She does add, "But neither do we."

This is similar to the cliché "let's agree to disagree." This brings back memories of when I would engage in conversations with strangers in the doctor's waiting room or in line at City Hall, or wherever the opportunity arose. I'd first start with small talk about the weather and some innocuous question about politics or current affairs. Then I would speak about Islamophobia, which they were always eager to speak about. Then in a soft manner I'd ask, "Do you think female genital mutilation is barbaric and should be outlawed?"

The response eight out of ten times was, "Well…it is hard to judge. It depends where it is being done."

It would usually become a heated conversation/argument/debate. I was accused of seeing the world in black and white, right and wrong. I would respond with: "But the little girl…"

They would say, "But it is their culture."

During my anti-Islam activities in 2014 at Dundas Square, I was confronted by a crowd of Muslims. I loudly asked a 20-year-old female Muslim who was attempting to put me in my place, "Can we say that the Islam in Saudi Arabia is the true Islam? What about the Islam in Sudan or Pakistan? Is that the true Islam?"

She replied, "What can we say is the true anything?"

I replied "So we cannot say what is the true Islam, we cannot say what is the false Islam."

She replied, "Yes."

I said, "Then ISIS, al-Qaeda could be the true Islam. Hamas or Hezbollah could be the true Islam?"

She fell silent.

Professor Manji says her reformed Islam is not necessarily the true Islam. It then follows that the other Islam is not necessarily the un-true Islam.

Professor Manji says, "We Muslims cannot play God with the lives of others."

What she is doing here is insinuating herself as the referee so that both sides will play "fair" by her rules. But the opposition, who is on a vastly superior footing to her, could not care less about Manji's rules. Do fundamentalists intend to play God? Who knows? However, Islamic doctrine tells us that they do intend to be the instruments to enforce Allah's will as they understand it. Imam Yasir Qadhi said, "There is a fine line between a pious Muslim and a fanatic terrorist." [51] Would a Muslim that kills a Muslim who is attempting to reform Islam be considered a terrorist or a true believer?

Manji says all sides should, with respect and civility, agree to disagree. Why would a pious Muslim pay attention to Manji, whom he views as deserving death? He would pay attention to the Muslim scholars, the aHadith and the Quran that instruct that people like Professor Manji should be killed. Being threatened with death by the Muslim community leaders is a long way from getting these

51 https://youtu.be/Kj-JkIoOO-Q

leaders to consider altering their religious beliefs because you say they should.

Professor Manji made a claim that some say demonstrates hubris:

> *The beauty of being in the position of reforming our fellow Muslims is that we come to see that worshiping one God, and not God's self-appointed ambassadors, compels us to defend human liberties. That of course means freedom of expression, freedom of conscience, non-violent freedom of thought.*

A Presupposition Buffet

Professor Manji tells us she is in a position to reform Muslims. Hospitals are filled with psychologists trying to reform people. Penitentiaries are filled with penologists trying to reform prisoners. In both these cases, success is not overwhelming; and that is captive populations that to some extent want to reform. Has Professor Manji ascertained whether Muslims are open to the idea of being reformed? We must take into account the fact that many Muslims are openly hostile to Professor Manji and call her a pervert. Will she overcome this with her bubbly personality and chutzpa and cajole Muslims into accepting her version of Islam? Anything is possible. After all, Oprah Winfrey's magazine gave Manji its first annual **Chutzpah Award** for "audacity, nerve, boldness and conviction."

There are many questions to ask Professor Manji regarding her claim to be in a position to reform Muslims. One, when does reforming transition to conversion therapy? Two, since Muslims want you dead, why do you think you can influence them?" But Bret Stephens did not ask this question.

Then there is the presupposition that "worshiping one God ... compels us to defend human liberties."

How does worshiping one God compel a person to defend human rights? I could say riding a bike compels us to believe in global warming. Riding a bike compels us forward; it does not compel a belief. Furthermore, is it the god you worship that compels you, or is it the worship of one god that compels you? Does that mean that if you worshiped two gods you would not be compelled to defend social justice?

Bret Stephens: *What are we to make of this clash of rights and identity politics?*

The Professor replies that the Islamic superiority complex leads some Muslims to believe that Western cultural and civic morals do not apply to them. So, no matter how unreasonable their demands, they expect to be accommodated. Professor Manji says that this behavior is wrong because the Quran does allow for versatility. However, there is a vital nuance that she is omitting or unaware of. The goal of Islam is fixed, but the means to achieve that goal is flexible.

An example that illustrates this is Muslim men engaging in anal intercourse, which is forbidden on pain of death.

In June of 2012, London-based Imam Abdullah Al-Khilaf said, concerning the **Widening Anus fatwa:**

> *The rule is that necessity makes the forbidden permissible. Something that is required in order to perform a duty becomes a duty in and of itself. No duty takes precedence over jihad.*

The reasoning is that sodomy enlarges the anus, thus allowing for more explosives to be packed in.[52]

52 https://www.memri.org/tv/london-based-shiite-cleric-abdallah-al-khilaf-

Do Not Let the Camel Put His Nose in Your Tent

There is no Islamic doctrine that enjoins Muslims to accommodate non-Muslims or to forgo Islamic rituals for the sake of accommodation or social harmony. In fact, Islamic doctrine, as well as modern Islamic teachings, help Muslims understand how Islamic ritual can be leveraged as a cultural imposition upon the host society. It has the effect of weakening the host culture's confidence, as well as promoting the Islamic culture as indigenous. The primary objective of NCCM, as stated in numerous ways on their website, is to induce the Canadian public to accept Islamic rituals and values as normative. One workshop is called "How to promote the hijab as the champion of feminism and human rights."

Professor Manji tells us the Quran permits flexibility. Permission to do something does not mean it will be done. All religions and political ideologies give flexibility for people to wake up at 4 a.m. and jog ten kilometers, stop eating sugar, or disconnect from social media. Human nature dictates that, at times, people want what they want, and they prefer not to compromise.

Voices That Prefer Not to Accommodate

Sheikh Abu Ameenah Bilal Philips:

> *Islam is a moral message. To implement that message is why you have jihad. But spilling blood and acquiring land is not the purpose of jihad.*[53]

---

wahhabi-fatwa-permits-sodomy-widen-anus-means-jihad

53 https://youtu.be/LH3UJUPZZDY

Sheik Suleman Anwar Bengarsa in 2010 at the Masjid Toronto:

> *If Muslims can walk into a place and establish Shari'ah without a drop of blood, then that is what they must do. Sometimes they did not have to engage in armed conflict. The people surrendered and accepted Islam.*

At a Friday sermon at Edmonton, Canada in February 2016, **Sheikh Shaban Sherif Mady** said:

> *The Prophet Mohammad told us that Constantinople would be conquered. This was the capital city of the Byzantine Empire. Today it is in Turkey. Turkey, Montenegro, all the way to Bosnia and Herzegovina and Serbia... all these countries were ruled by the rightly guided caliphate. It ruled about half of Europe, in the east, and the other half, in the west, the countries of al-Andalus: Spain, Portugal, and parts of France, all the way to the Ural Mountains. Constantinople will be conquered. It is the Prophet Mohammad who said so. And what was Constantinople? Just like the Vatican today, it was the capital of all the Christians in the world. It was conquered and became Turkey. The Hagia Sophia became a great mosque, where Allah is worshiped. The prophecies of the Prophet Mohammad came true. But some prophecies have not yet come true. Prophet Mohammad said that Rome would be conquered! Constantinople was conquered. Rome is the very heart of the Christian state.* [54]

For the Christians of Turkey, Egypt, and North Africa, interfaith bridge-building compromise was not on the table. Today, the West

54 https://youtu.be/7Kv_ReJDEWk

is well equipped with highly trained inter-religious bridge-building dialogue professionals.

Declarations About Hell?

> **Manji:** *Go with it. It doesn't mean that that they're going to go to Hell or you're going to go to Hell.*

Why would Muslims listen to a lesbian from Canada talking about Hell? She did say, reformers do not necessarily have the complete truth. The part of the truth they do not have could be the going to Hell part.

> **Manji:** *And the argument that I make in Love, Liberty and Allah is that if more people knew that there were those passages in the Quran about love and compassion, Muslims would be more tolerant.*

Manji does make this statement in her book. However, some will point out that her statement is not an argument. The Professor is using her book that contains an unsubstantiated statement as a source.

Mass Muslim Cultural Enrichment

Immigration to the West from the Middle East increased dramatically in the late 1960s. At the time, it was accepted that the Muslim immigrants were just like those from Hungary, Greece, Italy or Poland. This assumption is still widely held.

In the 1990s, mass migration from Middle Eastern countries increased considerably. The refugee crisis in 2015, arising from the war in Syria, brought millions of Muslims to Europe. A few years later, America's withdrawal from Afghanistan brought 123,000 more Muslim refugees to the US.

In her talk, Professor Manji said that mass migration must be practically faced because it is the new reality. She says this in connection with the Quebec niqab controversy (see Chapter 12), but never addresses the reality of Western citizens being killed by "misunderstanding" Muslim jihadists, the majority of whom, or their parents, were given asylum by the West. Perhaps this is outside her area of expertise. But one has to wonder how it affects the possibility of reforming Islam when there is a constant stream into the West of Muslims from the Third Word whose Islam is hostile to reform. Some will point to this as a case of shoveling sand against the tide.

> **Manji:** *You know it's easy to focus entirely on the negative because of course that's what gets the headlines.*

Is this an example of unconscious bias on the Professor's part? Are newspapers headlining Muslim terror, or is Muslim terror headline news? In various parts of the world, Sunnis blow up Shia mosques, and Shia blow up Sunni mosques. Is that one of the many realities of immigration that is arriving in the West? Will it cease being headline news?

Manji goes on:

> *The European Foundation for Democracy is currently building a network of reformist Muslims in Europe. They are being equipped to respond to fire bombers with civility and dignity and a love of individual liberty.*

Bret Stephens forgot to ask how this will stop the fire bombers.

Muslim Reformers' plan is to have specially trained social media brigades strategically deployed. At a moment's notice they can counter reporting that connects Islam to a fire bombing. I assume that includes bus bombings, nightclub shootings, and teacher beheadings. How does this reform Islam? But most importantly these media brigades help maintain inter-religious social harmony and prevent civic unrest.

If a Tree Falls in the Forest and No One Hears it …

> **Manji:** *Just because we're not reading about other Muslim reformers doesn't mean that they don't exist. We often assume, this is my experience, when we don't hear from them – largely because the media don't pay attention to the "good Muslims" who are saying "good things" – it must mean that they are not there.*

The Professor is implying that there could be Muslim reformers that the media has not reported on. That is possible. It is also possible the media does not report on them because they do not exist. Professor Manji tells us the "media don't pay attention to the good Muslims". Why does the professor think the existence of good Muslims is something newsworthy? Should we not assume all Muslims are good?

When the professor labels someone "good Muslims," by extension she labels someone else a "bad Muslim." This leads to "otherizing." Leaving that aside, however, these are malleable, subjective terms.

Should the social justice movement influence the standard from which good and bad are measured?

Since the 1970s, mainstream Islam has been building a network in Europe. Today, that network consists of 2,500 mosques in France, 2,500 mosques in Germany and a network of official and unofficial Shari'ah courts and thousands of madrassas throughout Europe. They are all connected with Egypt, Saudi Arabia, Turkey, Morocco, and Tunisia. Canada can now boast it has a mosque in the territory of Inuvik to service the growing Muslim population. This network is well funded by Muslim countries and to some extent by Western governments. How will Professor Manji's organization of well-meaning gentle souls fare in this contest to reform Islam? Many non-Muslims are under the impression that agreeing with and rooting for reformers is an action that will help in the reformation of Islam. Rational sports fans know that cheering for a team has no effect on the outcome of a game.

> **Manji:** *Muslim liberals do not step up to the plate, but conservative Imams do.*

Manji is conceding that mainstream Muslims and not reformers are driving the agenda. Typically, those who "step up to the plate" and drive the agenda will be victorious.

> **Manji:** *So, I would like to address how to transcend this ... because it is thinking about things strategically and then tactically... Bring them to the attention of journalists and equip them, these Muslim liberal reformists, to become savvy about engaging with the media.*

So, while reformers are engaging the media after a fire bombing, who is engaging Muslims in the worldwide Islamic network? Irshad Manji speaks in churches, synagogues, libraries and auditoriums filled with non-Muslims. But non-Muslims do not need to be reformed.

> *Manji: I know of a member of this liberal Muslim empowerment network that's being cultivated by the European Foundation for Democracy. A young man by the name of Ahmed. He is an Israeli Arab Muslim who now lives in Germany. He is working with Muslim youth boys in Germany to redefine the notion of honour.*

A nice young Arab man in Europe is going to attempt to amend Islamic doctrine and Arab tribal culture. Will this man contradict CAIR (the Council of American Islamic Relations), or NCCM, or CCI (Canadian Council of Imams), or ECI (European Council of Imams), or…? Will he have any effect in countering the message of Sheikh Bilal Philips? Will this boy's message stem the tide of **Al-Azhar University in Egypt**?

There are five thousand mosques in France and Germany. Ninety-seven percent of them are preaching mainstream Islamic doctrine. Pew research indicates that by 2050, the European Muslim population will be at least 35 million.[55]

> ***Manji:*** *He wants to take these boys as part of their graduation gift to Israel to show them what a pluralistic society can look like. He is also holding workshops with these young men about homophobia.*

55 https://www.ericbrazau.com/muslim-demographic-increase-europe/

So, this boy will take five other boys to Israel and hold workshops on homophobia and then what? Could this one boy repeat this four times a year? If he did this and he succeeded at a rate of 40%, that would be eight boys. Any amount of success is to be lauded and commended. But how does this affect the reality of mainstream Islam making progress in the West to the detriment of reform Islam?

Bret Stephens did not ask Professor Manji about IERA in juxtaposition to this man. There are two possible reasons. First, and most likely, Stephens has no knowledge of this organization. Second, this was not an interview but a pleasant conversation in the spirit of interfaith bridge-building dialogue.

Violent Jihad Tarnishes Islam's Image

Professor Manji closed her talk with the story of a young Muslim that was showering her with compliments. She suggested he tell his story to a newspaper in Bergen, Norway. The boy told her that he did not think any news outlet would do a story about him. Professor Manji told the audience she understood why a Muslim male would feel uncomfortable walking into a newspaper office.

She explained how life for Muslims in Europe is difficult because the fear of them is so high. They fear being asked to leave or being suspected of being a terrorist. Professor Manji flips the narrative and mocks Europeans who are fearful of Muslim males. She makes it clear that she sympathizes with Muslims' anxiety about the possibility of unfair or embarrassing treatment.

But let's compare that to what happened in the Netherlands on November 2, 2004. This was just two years after politician Pim Fortuyn was shot six times outside a media center in Hilversum, Holland, for his statements about Muslim immigrants. Dutch filmmaker and social activist Theo van Gogh was shot, stabbed seven times, then decapitated. All this was done in broad daylight by a young Muslim Moroccan in view of many witnesses. Similarly, in the Danish Cartoon Crisis of 2005, hundreds of thousands protested, leaving 250 dead and 800 wounded. In April 2009, a Muslim drove his car into a parade of the Dutch royal family. He killed eight and left ten injured. In June 2012, demonstrations against the film *Innocence of Muslims* claimed fifty lives. Professor Manji lightheartedly remarked about firebombing a newspaper office. And yet, in 2011, Muslims did firebomb the offices of Charlie Hebdo.

Professor Manji has a very amusing, whimsical personality. It gives her the ability to make serious, troubling issues that would otherwise come across as foreboding and ominous seem inconsequential and trivial. Manji ends this story by offering to introduce this young Muslim to reporters.

> *They will at least know that they can count on you to give comment the next time something awful happens in the name of Islam.*

As with the firebombing earlier, the Professor did not say if, but when. The Professor accepts that Muslim terror attacks in the West are inevitable. It would be useful to understand why Professor Manji thinks it is beneficial for some random Muslim to comment on misunderstanding Muslim terror attacks. Perhaps he is being trained to lead a Muslim reform love and compassion media brigade.

Some will connect Manji's comments to September 19, 2016 when, on a trip to New York City, London's Muslim Mayor Sadiq Khan said terror attacks are "part and parcel" of urban life, just hours after police foiled multiple jihadist terror plots in New York and New Jersey:

> *It is a reality, I'm afraid, that London, New York, other major cities around the world have got to be prepared for these sorts of things.* [56]

We conclude based on Pew Research reports that 87% of Muslims do not support terror attacks on civilians we can conclude 13%. Germany and France has a Muslim population of eleven million. 13% is 1.3 million individuals. We juxtapose this with progressive Muslim reformers, who number at most, 110.000 individuals.

56 https://www.dailymail.co.uk/news/article-3801018/Terror-attacks-parcel-living-big-city-claims-London-mayor-Sadiq-Khan.html

CHAPTER 11

THE TROUBLE WITH ISLAM

Professor Manji's book was well received by mainstream media and academia. On Amazon it has received 4 ½ stars from 300 reviews and has been translated into thirty languages.

This book started the rise of Irshad Manji's status as a beacon of hope that Islam could be something other than what mainstream Muslim leaders say it is.

When Did We Stop Thinking?

The above is the title of the third chapter from Manji's book. She poses a question to which there are several clear answers. The following is from a lecture uploaded to YouTube by Colorado Imam Karim AbuZaid. After that, we learn from the writings of Hizb ut-Tahrir.

Sheikh Karim AbuZaid:

This is the whole religion of Islam. That you make 'belief' of the unseen. What is 'belief?' Believe beyond any shadow of doubt. You're not skeptical and you don't try to use your intellect. When you employ that methodology of understanding or dealing with the unseen, this may lead you to leave Islam. [57]

Hizb ut-Tahrir:

Freedom of belief does not exist for Muslims. They are obliged to embrace the Islamic Akita (belief). It is not allowed for a Muslim to embrace any other creed such as Judaism, Christianity, capitalism or socialism, or any thought other than Islam. It is evident a Muslim is prohibited to accept the freedom of religion which capitalists call for. He is obliged to reject it and to challenge anyone who calls for it.

Hizb ut-Tahrir:

The prophet told us how to think, how to worship, what is acceptable, what is dignified… As to the individual, how to dress, what is hygiene, which hand to eat with, how to treat women, every aspect of trade, business, economy. There is a certain way to think when we are Muslims.

What is confusing is that Manji chose to name the chapter "When Did We Stop Thinking?" when the Quran clearly tells us. 5:101 – "O ye who believe! Ask not questions about things which, if made plain to you, may cause you to doubt."

Toronto Imam Syed Rizvi:

Ask questions in order to seek understanding. Do not ask questions in order to create confusion and then you get yourself into

57 https://youtu.be/sqLNAI5zzss

> *more complications... Don't ask questions which are not relevant... And if you still continue that habit of asking irrelevant questions* to Prophet Mohammad, while the Revelation is still coming, *you will be exposed in a way you wouldn't like.*[58]

Not thinking outside approved parameters is a fundamental aspect of mainstream Islamic doctrine and teaching. By asking this question, she is implying that Muslims not thinking is something new.

Should a Leopard Be Asked to Change Its Spots?

> *Instead of acknowledging a serious* ***problem with the guts of this religion,*** *we reflexively romanticize Islam.* (The Trouble with Islam, p.54)

The gut of something is its essence. How then does Professor Manji hope to reform Islam?

Manji tells us (Trouble with Islam) that in Toronto, an openly gay politician, whom she does not name, spoke against Islamophobia. She wrote that she hoped he expected reciprocal outrage from Muslims next time a gay club got firebombed.

Again, Professor Manji does not say *if* it is firebombed but *next time* it is firebombed.

We also know that the next time there is a Muslim terror attack everyone will be in shock and will display outrage. As with all events, people will become desensitized and adapt to a new reality. There could come a time when terrorism receives less coverage than the

58 *https://youtu.be/b2-CFnzewkg*

World Cup soccer matches, unless of course the number of dead exceeds one hundred. But then again, what is one hundred killed in a world of seven billion? Some argue that this is the price for the benefits of Muslim diversity. We must always keep in mind what interfaith bridge-building dialogue teaches us. The vast majority -- 87% of Muslims do not directly engage in violent Islamic terrorism._

A Sanctioned System of Discriminatory Provisions

On (Trouble with Islam) Professor Manji tells us that the Pact of Umar has been accepted as a divinely sanctioned system of discriminatory provisions. These provisions have been reinforced by Muslim legislatures and judges since the 9th century.

Since the **Pact of Umar** has taken on a divinely sanctioned system of discrimination, Islamophobes will say the religion of Islam is discriminatory. How does this affect the Canadian Islamophobia motion M-103? This motion set many wheels turning. It is the basis of many government programs and bureaucracies devoted to the "elimination of anti-Islam bias."

Professor Manji:

> *Under Muslim rule, Jews and Christians have historically bought their protection. They have paid for their lives by handing over a poll tax.* (The Trouble with Islam)

However, Professor Manji tells us when the general peace didn't appear to be jeopardized, Prophet Mohammad *PBUH* did not collect the head tax, jizyia. The following 5 Quran translations help contextualize our understanding.

Qurans 9:29:

Fight those who do not believe in Allah or in the Last Day and who do not consider unlawful what Allah and His Messenger have made unlawful and who do not adopt the religion of truth from those who were given the Scripture and:[59]

a. *Pay the jizyia and feel themselves subdued and humiliated, or*
b. *until they give the jizyia willingly while they are humbled, or*
c. *until they pay the tribute readily, being brought low, or*
d. *until they pay the jizya with willing submission, and feel themselves subdued, or*
e. *until they pay the tax in acknowledgment of superiority and they are in a state of subjection*

Many people base their opinion of Islam upon their understanding of the Quran. Points a, b, c, d and e are all similar yet have subtle differences. For example, acknowledging the superiority of others is not the same as being brought low. Willing submission is not the same as being subjugated against one's will. Muslim scholars and those who engage in interfaith dialogue agree that these differences, while at times imperceptible, when acknowledged lead to successful interfaith/religious bridge-building dialogue. Success in the context of interfaith bridge-building dialogue is defined as agreeing to agree on points that all agree to. It is also agreeing to agree there are points

59 https://corpus.quran.com/translation.jsp?chapter=9&verse=29

of disagreement and agreeing to continue engaging in interfaith bridge-building dialogue.

Support for Head Tax Confirmed in Toronto

The book *Human Rights in Islam* that is distributed at no cost, to the public, by the Toronto dawa'h group at Dundas Square, advocates charging a head tax.

> *The non-Muslim residents of an Islamic state are required to pay a minimal tax called 'Jizyah' which is a specific type of head-tax collected from individuals who do not accept Islam and desire to keep their religion while living in an Islamic state and under Islamic rule.*

We learn that "fundamentalist" Islam is being faithfully and diligently propagated by pious Muslims in Toronto, across North America, Europe and Australia. We learn that based on the example of Prophet Mohammad *PBUH* a Muslim ruler can decide to decrease or cancel the head tax; one would assume the humiliation that accompanies the payment would also be canceled.

CHAPTER 12

ALLAH, LIBERTY AND LOVE

When Manji wrote Allah Liberty Love she was a Professor at New York University where she joined NYU's **Robert F. Wagner Graduate School of Public Service** to create the Moral Courage Project. This is an initiative to teach young people how to speak truth to power within their own communities. The book *Allah, Liberty and Love* established Manji as a leader of the Muslim reform movement. Many agree that if Islam is to be reformed and liberalized, much of the Islamic doctrine must be reinterpreted. To do this Professor Manji relies on her interpretation of the concept of itjihad. We begin our journey into this seminal work by examining Manji's application of itjihad.

> *Ijtihad equals jihad, a struggle of the mind that implies freedom to ask questions, sometimes uncomfortable ones.* (Allah, Liberty and Love, p.2)

This is ijtihad from the perspective of Professor Manji. Below is the mainstream Muslim understanding of itjihad as I understand it:

Itjihad: A Muslim woman comes across a man she is unrelated to hanging off a cliff. She can save his life. To do so she would have to remove her hijab to use as a rope and possibly touch hands with the man as well as speak to him. All this would take place without the presence of a chaperone. In Islam, none of this is permissible. However, because a man's life could be saved, it raises the issue of Musleha (committing a small sin for the greater good). If there is no Islamic doctrine or past ruling (jurisprudence) dealing with this precise circumstance, itjihad comes into play. The approved highly respected scholars, after careful deliberation, will render a verdict.

Itjihad is a ruling upon circumstances that have never before arisen and therefore have never been ruled upon. Changing a ruling or an accepted practice is considered an act of bid'ah (religious innovation). Engaging in bid'ah garners a severe punishment.

Democracy vs. Reality

In March 2011, Pakistan's minorities minister Shahbaz Bhatti was shot dead. In January that year, Mr. Bhatti told the BBC he would defy the death threats he had received from Islamist militants for his efforts to reform the blasphemy law. It was reported that the assassins left leaflets signed "Taliban Al-Qaeda Punjab" that described Bhatti as a "Christian infidel." Months earlier, Salman Taseer, the Governor of Punjab, who was also working to reform the blasphemy law, was gunned down by one of his bodyguards.

Since the assassinations, the Pakistani Government has unambiguously decided to lay off the blasphemy laws, its ministers hinting privately that it was a hornets' nest best left untouched. [60]

60 https://www.bbc.com/news/world-south-asia-12617562

Reformers tell us that these murders do not represent the true Islam or the teaching of the Prophet Mohammad *PBUH*. The explanation then is that these assassins are Muslims that misunderstand. However, some in the Ummah (World Muslim community) see them as martyrs for the cause of Allah. This was also the view of some Muslims in Holland and in France when Theo Van Gogh and Samuel Paty were beheaded. Is it possible that mainstream Muslims who support jihadists and venerate them as martyrs for the cause of Allah are misunderstanding Islam?

In 2022, Salman Rushdie was stabbed on a stage in New York by a man born in California. People have been accused of using this incident to bolster their rhetoric that Islam wants to destroy the West. This is a fallacy. This right-wing rhetoric is conflating individual Muslims with the religion of Islam. What they probably mean to say is that some Muslims born in America want to destroy America and or Western civilization. It is erroneous to judge all Muslims based on the actions of one Muslim. It would however be accurate if they said "Islamic doctrine tells us…"; or "the teachings of the Muslim leader instruct Muslims to…"

> *Militants and even mainstream Muslims have curdled Islamic faith into an ideology of fear.* (Allah, Liberty and Love, p. 4)

Manji tells us "Islam is what Muslims make it." (Trouble with Islam) Since Muslims have curdled Islam into a religion of fear, how long will it take reformers to reform it into a religion of love and compassion?

> *Faith does not forbid exploration. It's dogma by definition that is threatened by questions.* (Allah liberty Love)

Muslim scholars fully agree with Professor Manji. They make it clear that anyone who asks annoying or "smart-ass" questions will be severely punished.

> *Muslims are monotheist. To be a monotheist, you must accept that only Allah knows the full truth ... so it is an act of faith to create societies in which we can disagree without physical harm from the other. To devote myself to one God is to defend liberty.* (Allah liberty love xxxx)

"To devote myself to one God is to defend liberty": This is two concepts smashed together. One idea has no bearing on the other. If someone said "to devote myself to multiple gods is to defend liberty" it would be nonsensical. You could just as easily be a dictator who devotes himself to one God.

"Disagree without physical harm": That will certainly benefit those to whom harm is being done. Those that are doing might prefer not to stop.

Are Arabic Culture and Islam the Same?

> *Muslims gave the world mocha coffee and the guitar and possibly the expression "Olé" from the Arabic word "Allah."* (Allah Liberty Love)

There is debate in Musicology as to the origins of the guitar. The following Islamic teaching and doctrine sheds light on this.

Sheik Bilal Philips:

> *Music as we know it today, produced by wind and stringed instruments, is haram* [forbidden]. *When we look at the*

> *tradition of the* **early scholars of Islam** they made all kinds of statements against it. Some scholars *refer to music as the Quran of Shatan.* [61]

Islam Q&A:

> *A piano is a musical instrument, so it comes under the heading of the texts which forbid musical instruments and forbid listening to them. The evidence for that has been explained in previous answers.*
>
> *If a person is employed to move household goods and finds musical instruments among them, it is not permissible for him to move them…* [62]
>
> *There is a proven text concerning the prohibition of musical instruments, as in the hadith of Abu Maalik al-Ash'ari…*[63]

It is hard to imagine how Professor Manji could believe Muslims invented the guitar.

> *I am calling to get rid of the elitism that cements a pattern* (Allah, Liberty and Love, p.41). *Get rid of submissiveness among Muslims.*

If we refer to Arabic language dictionaries, we find that the meaning of the word "Islam" is: *submission,* humbling oneself, and obeying commands and heeding prohibitions *without objection,*

---

61 *https://youtu.be/aFwhkB-56sA*

62 *https://islamqa.info/en/answers/99979/one-who-is-employed-to-move-haraam-things-such-as-musical-instruments*

63 *https://islamqa.info/en/answers/169673/a-specious-argument-about-the-prohibition-of-musical-instruments-and-the-response-thereto*

sincerely worshipping Allah alone, believing what He tells us and having faith in Him.

[64] To be submissive to Allah is essential to being a Muslim. After the death of the Prophet Mohammad *PBUH,* several tribes preferred not to be submissive to Islam. This is known as the Wars of Ridda. Those tribes that wanted to leave Islam and revert back to their religions and customs were killed.

Sheikh Yusuf al-Qaradawi, based in Egypt, was the chairman of the International Union of Muslim Scholars:

> *If they had gotten rid of [the] apostasy punishment, Islam wouldn't exist today; Islam would have ended [after] the death of the Prophet, PBUH. So, according to* ***Abi Kulaba's*** *narration, this verse means the apostates, and many aHadith, not only one or two, but many, narrated by a number of Mohammad's companions state that any apostate should be killed.*

Islam Is Far Reaching

Professor Manji tells us a story (Allah, Liberty and Love, p.41) about a German Muslim woman that placed an interfaith authorization notice before her father, uncles, and brother. This authorization was provided by an Imam that allowed this woman to marry a Christian.

Interestingly, it was not placed before her mother, aunts and sisters. This girl did not present these men with the German law, EU law or human rights laws.

---

64 https://islamqa.info/en/answers/10446/

Numerous Islamic scholars and aHadith make it clear that a Muslim woman must never be permitted to marry a non-Muslim.

Sheikh Bilal Philips:

> *On the basis of* ***protecting the woman and her religion,*** *the children and their religion... This is why Islam does not allow a Muslim woman to marry [anyone] other than a Muslim man. It is not to oppress her; it is to protect her.* ***It is to protect the generations to come. To protect the religion of Islam.*** [65]

Imam Shabbir Ally:

> *It is well known and it is classified and codified in Islamic textbooks...* *And their great contribution to societies would have been get married, have children. They* ***increase the number of the tribe.*** *The tribe became larger and stronger. So each individual was contributing something to the growth of the tribe. And women in particular, that would have been a great contribution to their tribes by getting married early and having children.* [66]

Hadith:

> *It is absolutely* **not permissible under any circumstances** in Islamic law (*Shari'ah) for a non-Muslim man to marry a Muslim woman. They are not lawful (wives) for the unbelievers, nor are the unbelievers lawful (husbands) for them...* **(Al-Mumtahina:10)**

65 *https://www.youtube.com/watch?v=5-7F1jbVEy0*

66 *https://www.ericbrazau.com/islam-child-bride-pregnancy/*

Men can marry non-Muslims because the children will be Muslim. A non-Muslim father could raise his children as something other than Muslim. As Imam Shabbir Ally said, this weakens the Muslim tribe.

A Good Deed is Not an Ideology

> *Another Albanian Muslim testifies that she and her husband sheltered Jews.* (Allah, Liberty and Love, p.45)

There are stories of Jews saved by Germans. Nazi doctrine on Jews is clear. It is not affected by the actions of people. Islamic doctrine is also clear. There are also multitudes of Imams in the West who preach about killing Jews. Such cases are clearly documented.

Imam Sayyid Al-Ghitawi, Friday *khutba* (sermon), Montreal Quebec 2012: [67]

> *Oh Allah, destroy the accursed Jews. Oh Allah, show us the black day you inflict upon them. Oh Allah, kill them one by one. Do not leave a single one of them. Oh Allah, turn their children into orphans and their women into widows. Oh Allah, make them suffer adversities..*

California Sheikh Ammar Shahin, March 21, 2021:

> *Judgment day will not come until the Muslims fight the Jews. And the Jews hide behind stones... We don't say if it is in Palestine or another place. It does not say Oh Pakistani, oh Afghan, oh Indian. No, it will say: Oh Muslim. Oh Allah, count them and one by one annihilate them down to the very last one.* [68]

67 https://vimeo.com/580454604

68 https://youtu.be/GX5tAI4u6OY

The quote below is an excerpt from the prayer repeated 17 times a day by all Muslims. The following Imams Osman Haji Madad from Edmonton Alberta; Imam Musleh Khan, the Toronto Police Muslim Chaplain; Yusuf Badat Ex- Vice Chair, CCI; Sheikh Mashoor Hassan, Toronto Mosque:

> *Not the path of those who have incurred your anger or the path of those who have gone astray. Who are these people that Allah is referring to? The first group has been identified by the Prophet Mohammad as Yahoud (the Jews).Second group Prophet Mohammad has identified as the Nazarenes (Christians).* [69]

Some warn we must not to take words out of context, thus misrepresenting the intended meaning. However, others will say these words are clear in their meaning and need no context.

What effect will this have on the Muslim reform movement?

> *Reform-minded Muslims are not yet leaping out of the closets* (Allah, Liberty and Love, p.50)

Professor Manji tells us that there are not many reform-minded Muslims jumping to join the movement. It could be that, unlike Professor Manji, who some say, lives high in an ivory tower, most people are exposed to the realities of the community. Those who actively and openly support reforming Islam are at a minimum in danger of harassment, if not serious bodily harm. To say that Islam needs reformation is interpreted as an insult to Prophet Mohammad *PBUH* who revealed the perfect complete religion in the

69 https://youtu.be/YVQZLgzwl3o

perfect way. To suggest otherwise is blasphemous. Blasphemy is severely punished.

Toronto **Imam Jawed Anwar** wrote:

> *Muslims can tolerate anything… But whenever someone insults Prophet Mohammad, they always react, they get revenge. They cannot control their sentiments. The word tolerance doesn't apply here. The Muslim community will give warning. But if they do not abstain and ignore the collective demands of the Muslims, some young blood comes forward to make a score.* The non-Muslim world, the *courts, convicted and hangs them, but in the eyes of Muslims they are martyrs* [70]

Toronto **Imam Shabbir Ally**:

> *There are classical books* written that explain the religion of Islam. And these classical interpretations of Islam make it so objectionable to criticize God or the *Prophet or the scriptures of Islam, to the extent that they prescribe the death penalty for the critic.* [71]

Colorado **Imam Karim AbuZaid**:

> *Someone is insulting Mohammad… The whole Ummah is rising, saying we cannot take that! So,* ***why are we blamed*** *[for beheading Samuel Paty], rebuked* ***for showing this love?*** [72]

---

70 *https://www.as-seerah.com/Blasphemy-of-the-Prophet-Right-to-Revenge-1_308.html*

71 https://youtu.be/Vu-V2oOJ_l8

72 https://youtu.be/L4uMcGEUz4g

Skeptics of the reform movement argue that if reformers are afraid to step forward to be counted then it is possible very few of them actually exist.

Transitioning Identity

In the West, it is taken for granted that people are free to be and believe what they want. But not all people are free to define themselves or choose their preferred community. Hence Professor Manji's remark about identity:

> *Community doesn't have to be defined by a prefabricated identity that is assigned to you.* (Allah, Liberty and Love, p.56)

Professor Manji is correct – it does not have to be this way. However, several women in North America and Europe with assigned Muslim identities have attempted to redefine themselves. This resulted in their being killed by their close relatives. Can this be taken as a warning to other Muslims who are thinking of transitioning?

> *Arab leaders for the most part believe conformity is priority number one, as if community cannot tolerate individuality. Even in communal prayer, you don't need to surrender your individuality.* ***Abdullah Ahmid An-Naim****, a professor of human rights at Emory University, made this point to me during a public discussion about moral courage in March 2008. He said: "When I stand in prayer as a Muslim, I stand in the huge line of people, yet each one of us is praying as himself or herself. I don't know why people get so nervous about the difference and*

> *disagreement... each of us is an individual. What is bad is violence."* (Allah Liberty Love)

Manji asked if this concept of praying as an individual goes against the concept of one global Ummah.

> *He replied with a gleam in his eye that the concept of one Ummah is a myth.* (Allah Liberty Love)

He also said that sometimes Muslims overemphasize uniformity to hide disunity.

The Emory Professor tells us he does not understand what people get nervous about. The implication seems to be that because he does not understand the nervousness, it is irrational. He does not address the fact that Muslims frequently do commit violence over differences and disagreements. The Danish cartoonists, journalists at Charlie Hebdo, artist Molly Norris, and teachers in France are nervous. Has that nervousness spread to other European countries with Muslim communities? According to Professor *Abdullah Ahmid An-Naim* they should not be nervous. But he does not make a case for why.

Professor Manji tells us that Akbar Ladak said:

> *I will not shrink from the fight against Islamic fanaticism.*

This statement confirms that Islam contains elements of fanaticism. What is not known is the size of those elements? Dr. Jasser tells us that radical Islam is gaining popularity (Battle Souls Islam, p. 123, 134, 149, 206). This then contradicts Canada's M-103 that states Islam is a peaceful religion and that those who associate violence with Islam are guilty of Islamophobia. In Canada as of 2022,

Islamophobia is not adjudicated in a criminal court. https://legal-project.org/issues/canada-hrc

Reformer and Fundamentalist Agree About Fanaticism

Imam Syed Soharwardy founding member of CCI:

> *Basically, there are US organizations operating in Canada. One is called AlMaghrib Institute; the other is called AlKauthar Institute. Both work in universities, not in mosques. Both give lectures. Both organize seminars. They are the ones who brainwash these young kids in lectures. Their topic[s are] very normal. The shoe bomber in the United States attended AlMaghrib Institute lectures.*

Imam Yasir Qadhi uploaded a sermon in July 2022 eulogizing his mentor and the founder of AlMaghrib Institute. He tells us that AlMaghrib was the forerunner in utilizing Western techniques and technology to ensure the next generation of Muslim youth remains faithful and loyal to Islam and the cause of Allah. Imam Qadhi explains that he alone, with this method, has taught over a hundred thousand Muslim students in North America, Europe and Australia. In his eulogy, he says how Sheikh al-Shareef saw that the best way to influence youth was on the college campus. [73]

Toronto Imam Soharwardy concurs with Imam Akbar Ladak that radical, fanatic Islam is a reality.

---

73 https://www.youtube.com/watch?v=Pz012wgsjUs

Integrity is a Luxury

Professor Manji tells us the following regarding the Prophet Mohammad *PBUH*:

> *Feeling the heat of a few initial converts and riding resentment, the Prophet Mohammad PBUH made a strategic decision: he diluted his message to curry favour with Meccans.* (Allah, Liberty and Love, p.80)
>
> *Desperate to be heard, he drained his mission of its meaning.* (Allah Liberty Love)
>
> *Fear of being stigmatized by his community led Prophet Mohammad PBUH to compromise primary principles.* (Allah Liberty Love)

Many upon reading this will be surprised if not shocked that someone could say such a thing about the Prophet of Islam. It would then be natural to dismiss what Professor Manji is saying. After all, she is not an Imam. But Imam Yasir Qadhi said something with a similar meaning when giving a talk to a packed auditorium in Washington D.C. Sep 2013: https://youtu.be/ZCEz_kIe6WU

> *Scholars and clerics need to understand their responsibility is more than just preaching the truth. It is tempering the truth with wisdom. And brothers and sisters, let me be very explicit here, I myself have learned from my mistakes. Two decades ago, I as well gave inflammatory lectures and speeches. I said things that still haunt me to this day. [Kill Christians and Jews*

> *and take their property.] It was a younger version of me. I can excuse myself that I was 21 years old.*[74]

Many people believe that, unlike politics, religion is the unfettered truth spoken with no intent to manipulate the person hearing the message. In this regard, Professor Irshad Manji and Imam Yasir Qadhi are in agreement. Those considered Islamophobes will use this to suggest that Muslim leaders engaging in interfaith bridge-building dialogue are biding time until they have sufficient resources.

Sheikh Hakim Quick:

> *What is our situation as an Ummah? We find ourselves in a very critical time. We have huge numbers: over 26% of the Earth's population. Sixty percent of Muslims are young people. We have strategic positions all over the world. We have some of the richest people on earth.* [75]

Imam Abdool Hamid:

> *Islam does not want to take over for the sake of taking over... However,* ***changes will have to be made****. So, it may seem* ***from one perspective that Islam took*** *over, so to speak.* [76]

Combining the voices of these leading senior Muslim scholars with others in the Muslim community could lead Islamophobes to conclude there is a conspiracy being hatched. However, a conspiracy is an unlawful, harmful plan formulated in secret by two or more

---

74 *https://news.acdemocracy.org/american-muslim-scholars-statements-on-the-spiritual-filth-of-the-jews-christians/*

75 *https://youtu.be/aOYzYnfkDLw*

76 *https://youtu.be/K-91RRLwEhQ*

persons There are two simple arguments to dissuade people from this thought. First, the Muslim community does not see supplanting secular governments with the Shari'ah as unlawful or harmful. Second, none of this is being formulated in secret.

Conservative Prophet Mohammad *PBUH* Represents the Majority

> *Still, lots of us feel inadequate to the task because liberal interpretations of the prophet, as anything Islamic, are so much harder to come by than conservative ones. (*Allah, Liberty and Love, *p.83)*

Is Professor Manji is telling us that the vast majority of Muslims understand that conservative Islam is the Islam of Prophet Mohammad *PBUH?*

What then will be the basis for reformers to convince Muslims that their interpretation and understanding of Islam and Prophet Mohammad *PBUH* for the last 1400 years is wrong? Are mainstream fundamentalists Muslims wrong because Professor Manji and the reformers are right?

It is astonishing to think that a girl from Brampton, Ontario has a better grasp of Islam than the Companions *MABPWT* or writers of the aHadith or the author of *Garden of the Righteous* (an extremely popular compilation of authentic aHadith from the six major collections: Bukhari, Muslim, Abu Dawood, Tirmidhi, An-Nisai and Ibn Majah) or the Imams that advise Al-Qaeda or the Taliban or the Canadian Council of Imams or the European Imam Council. But even if we accept that Manji is right and the Muslim associations and councils are wrong, what will that change? If I am struck by a car and killed while crossing at a cross walk, it will be noted that I had the right of way and the driver was in the wrong. But being in the right does not change the fact that I am dead.

> *More than 80% of Muslims are non-Arab. Arab is assumed to be the authentic Islam. This wouldn't be so much an issue if Islam's leaders used religion to sanctify the best aspects of daily Arabic life. (*Allah, Liberty and Love, *p.90)*

Perhaps the Professor could be specific about these "best aspects of daily Arab life." Arab culture, according to many notable scholars, consisted of constant blood vendettas, extreme chronic drunkenness, gambling, and tribal warfare. When dealing with fellow humans, ethics was not a concept. To the Arabs, the only restraint on cruelty or barbarity was fear of retribution from the opposing tribe. The code of tribalism involved protecting your own tribesman, regardless of circumstances. Example of this is women that covered were recognized as belonging to Islam and were therefore not molested [77]

Dr. Jasser said that "the poison of Muslim tribalism did follow them to America." (Battle Souls Islam, p.159) Is this what he was referring to?

> *The Muslim student had been granted anonymity because he feared his words could bring him into serious conflict with Muslim religious authorities. Detect a theme? Fear, yes, but it is*

77 https://www.ericbrazau.com/toronto-imam-women-that-are-covered-recognized-will-not-be-molested/

> *also the low expectations of fellow Muslims and the high defense against possible retaliations. (*Allah, Liberty and Love, *p.93)*

The above quote is in reference to a Harvard student that complained about the university's Muslim chaplain that endorsed the death penalty for apostates.

Professor Manji references low expectations. Muslims acting violently is an experienced reality, so low expectations are to be expected. After all, Professor Manji did tell us Islam has been "curdled into an ideology of fear." (Allah Liberty Love) Islamophobes say Islam always was a religion of fear and hate.

Conflicting Apostasy Messages

Professor Irshad Manji wants people to understand that Islam as conveyed by Prophet Mohammad *PBUH* was a personal spiritual matter. To bolster this point, she cites an Egyptian cleric:

> *Egypt - Shaikh Gomaa concluded that a Muslim may adopt another religion ... Pointed to several verses: 109:6 - 18:29 - 2-256*
>
> *109.6 – For you is your religion, for me is my religion.* (Allah, Liberty and Love p.93)

In a somewhat contradictory fashion, Sheikh Gomaa, when replying to a question about apostasy, did say that it is a very serious sin. He also answered that belief in democracy is kufr. [78]

Being called a kufr in a Muslim context means a willful stubbornness to reject truth and sow discord that leads to insurrection.

78 https://eshaykh.com/search/?q=apostacy

In most cases insurrectionists are executed and those who sow discord are crucified.

Islamic scholars agree that the conciliatory verses were revealed by Prophet Mohammad *PBUH* when Islam was in the minority, with no political or military power in Medina. That changed with the conquest of Mecca and the Pact of Umar. This pact has been covered in previous chapters. It allows Jews and Christians to retain their religion if they pay the jizyia and feel themselves subdued and humiliated.

Quran 18:29:

> *Let him believe indeed we have prepared for the wrong doers a fire whose walls will surround them. And if they call for relief, they will be relieved with water like murky oil, which scalds their faces. Wretched is the drink and evil is the resting place.*

Missing prayer makes a Muslim a wrong doer.

Imam Mohammad Hoblos:

> *My brothers and sisters let me tell you something – and understand this as fact. In the eyes of Allah, the murderer, the adulterer, the fornicator and the one who drinks alcohol, who all of these sins on a daily basis but prays is better in the sight of Allah [than] the one who commits none of these sins but doesn't pray. So you say: "Yeah, I'm a good guy." You are worse than a murderer, you are worse than a rapist, in the eyes of Allah.*[79]

79 *https://vimeo.com/394568333*

Sheikh Yasir Qadhi gave an interview days after the beheading of Samuel Paty in which he touched on the two sides of conciliation:

> *We have to acknowledge that we do have two sets of principles or paradigms depending on our context... There is indeed a Mecca phase and a Medina phase... Obviously in the Medina phase Muslims have political power and there is a very different set of rules.* [80]
>
> *2:256: There shall be no compulsion in acceptance of the religion.*

In 2010, **Imam Suleiman Bengharsa** gave an intimate lecture to a group of advanced students in Toronto. Following is a partial transcript of a video uploaded to YouTube that speaks directly to the conciliatory verse in the Holy Quran:

It is important you make the non-Muslim feel like he ***needs to become Muslim*** *in order for him* ***to have equal rights***. [81]

What the Imam is saying is supported by the Pact of Umar that codified inferior status to non-Muslims.

Muslim reformers state in their declaration, "We stand for universal peace, love and compassion." They also reject violent jihad and prefer secular governance, freedom of speech and religion. Many people throughout history have had preferences. For example, the people of Byzantine Empire preferred to remain Christian.

> *[In] this area we call Turkey there [were] no Muslims, there was no Islam, right? ... It was a result of jihad. Muslims came with the sword, and established Shari'ah.*

80 https://youtu.be/hi8gzaeMqUU

81 https://youtu.be/URqm7p97nBA

> *Some Muslims say, "Oh, Islam was never spread by the sword." That's a blatant lie. It was spread by the sword many times. The implementation of Shari'ah was spread by the sword.*

Imam Shabbir Ally:

> *ISIS published its manifesto in which it cites verses of the Quran, the aHadith and rulings of Muslim scholars, and citations from tasveer, commentary on the Quran, to justify their actions.*

Both Imam Shabbir Ally and Imam Suleiman Bengharsa, unequivocally contradict the narrative propagated by virtually all leaders of the Western world. After 9/11, George Bush told Americans Islam is a religion of peace, as did Tony Blair. But no Western leader gushes over Islam quite like Canadian Prime Minister Justin Trudeau:

National broadcast:

> *Canadians are quick to point out that ISIS is wrong that Islam is not incompatible with the Western secular democracy [in] a free place like Canada.*

Speaking at a Montreal mosque:

> *For me, this moment of Ramadan is a time to reflect on the values of empathy, generosity and compassion, charity and also discipline. They are not just Muslim values but Canadian values.*

Response to a heckler at a Muslim fundraiser:

> *Brother, is it not the words of the Quran that say when someone speaks to you in anger you answer them with words of peace?*

House of Parliament:

> *The Quran tells us the true servants of the most merciful are those who behave gently and with humility, honour, and whenever the foolish quarrel with them they reply with words of peace.*

It is difficult to understand how Justin Trudeau can believe he has a better understanding of Islam than these two Imams. Shabbir Ally is the president of the Canadian International Dawa'h and the author of ten books on Islam. He has an MA & PhD in Islamic studies from the University of Toronto. Imam Suleiman Bengharsa lectures across North America and was the Muslim Chaplain in a Maryland prison.

Islam and Tribalism

> *Take the Pakistani women. They told the head nurse at a New York hospital that they can't accept intervention because their culture sanctions the battering of women by men... If these women are capable of dreaming that life can be free of welts and bruises, then with more choices they'll possibly make new decisions. ... These women do not have freedom to know themselves as individuals; for them tribal identity poses as personal integrity.* (Allah, Liberty and Love, p.106)

Here Professor Manji tells us that tribalism and culture can be a person's identity. Interestingly, evolutionary psychologists have said that preferring one's own kinfolk and ethnicity is a natural human trait.[82] Being among one's close family releases a certain love hor-

82 https://pubmed.ncbi.nlm.nih.gov/29563059/

mone that is the same as that which is released between infants and their mothers.[83] Humans have evolved over millennia to have strong, deep-seated bonds to their family to the exclusion of others. It also means that as Canada becomes more diverse, it will see an increase in the number and size of ethnic and religious diverse enclaves. Muslim leaders do instruct Muslims to live among themselves and create Muslim sanctuaries where Islamic laws and values are the norm. They also warn against integration.

Diversity Professor – People Prefer Their Own Kind

Will Kymlicka is the Research Chair of the Philosophy Department at Queen›s University in Kingston, Canada, where he has taught since 1998. He said that people have a "deep bond" to their culture and ethnicity. (P.87 Canada in Decay Ricardo Duchesne)

Given what Professors Manji and Kymlicka tell us, people from Pakistan, Somalia or Afghanistan will be happiest living in a Muslim area with people of the same ethnic and cultural background. As more Muslim Pakistanis, Somalis and Bangladeshis come to Canada, it will become easier for several little Pakistans, Bengals or Somalias to be created. We also have Islamic leaders encouraging Muslims to create their own separate Islamic enclaves. This is encouraged by the Canadian government, as in the case of Muslim-only subsidized housing units. Those on the Right say this ensures sectarian tribal conflict or balkanization comes to Canada. Others say this diversity makes Canada stronger and contributes to cultural enrichment.[84]

---

83 https://pubmed.ncbi.nlm.nih.gov/23769813/

84 https://globalnews.ca/news/2187517/toronto-city-councillor-says-muslim-only-subsidized-housing-is-acceptable/

Right-wingers concede that Canada in the recent past had Italian, Polish, Greek and German ghettos. They argue that the difference that makes all the difference was that all these nationalities lived within a Western European Christian ethos. For the most part, community leaders embraced Canadian culture because Canadian culture was Western and Christian. On the other hand, Muslim leaders tell the community to reject Canadian values because they are Western and Christian. A Polish father might prefer his daughter marry a Pole, but he could very likely approve of an upstanding Italian boy. A Polish girl would never consider the possibility her family will strangle her for falling in love with an Italian. Muslim girls in the West have been murdered for dating non-Muslims.

Reforming the West to Accommodate the East

> *These questions should help Muslims and non-Muslims think clearly about how to reform ourselves and the greater good.* (Allah, Liberty and Love, p.111)

Professor Manji has appointed herself as the arbiter of the "greater good." When she says "non-Muslims need think clearly about how to reform," what aspect of non-Muslim Canadian history or culture does she wish to start adapting and modifying? Right-wingers argue that those who are immigrating to the West should do all the adapting and reforming. Otherwise at some point Canada will cease to be Canada and will be more like Afghanistan, Bangladesh or Somalia. There would then be no reason to emigrate from Somalia to Canada since Canada now resemble Somalia

Appreciating Cultural Norms

Professor Manji tells us (Allah, Liberty and Love, p.137) that in Jordan, a young Muslim man pumped bullets into his sister after a brother-in-law raped her. The media reported that he said, "Tradition and society inflict things on us. This is our society. This is how we were brought up and it will never change."

People can be very loyal to a culture, especially if they see it as part of their heritage passed down to them by their forefathers. It is an emotional attachment. When people immigrate to the West, they add their culture to the overall diversity of cultural enrichment. Some ask if it is acceptable to reject aspects of other cultures. Multiculturalists and those that participate in interfaith bridge-building say that to refuse certain cultures or aspects of cultures is **cultural elitism**.

Benefitting from the System

Toronto Imam Syed Regeah:

> *With five hundred thousand Muslims you can create the most powerful lobby in Canada... If we put our resources together – work as an Ummah [Muslim nation].We are here, we may as well benefit from the system they have here. What can you do with unity [a voting bloc]? You can change a lot. You can change the foreign policy of this country.* [85]

In London on July 7th 2005, four Muslims killed 52 and maimed and wounded hundreds by blowing up the London Underground. Professor Manji tells us that the leader of this terrorist cell, Mohammad

85 *https://youtu.be/-CcfHSOIygI?t=100*

Sidique Khan, may have felt resentful of Western foreign policy. (Allah, Liberty and Love, p.146)

What then does Professor Manji propose Western nations do in order to alleviate the resentment Muslims feel toward Western foreign policy? Islamophobes point to the two examples above and claim that Muslims are taking advantage of the system to infiltrate and build a fifth column.

Far-reaching conspiracy-minded individuals have speculated that Muslim leaders will announce, in the near future, that from this day forward, in our area or zone, we live by Shari'ah. Is this even remotely possible?

Let's consider the book *Garden of the Righteous* (***Riyad-us-Saliheen* by Imam al-Nawawi**). It is a primary resource for all Muslims. It is held in the highest regard as a book of the most authenticated Hadith.

> *It is a duty for Muslims to wipe out disbelief and instill the banner of Islam over the entire world. The objective of jihad warrants that one must struggle against kufr (disbelief) and shirk polytheism. Jihad has to continue until this objective is achieved... the jihad will continue till the day of resurrection...*
>
> *This Hadith strongly refutes the people who distort the Islamic concept of jihad and hold that Islam preaches defensive war only.*
>
> *...set them on the path of worship of Allah, and to provide a just and equitable society. Wherever in the world there is tyranny, ignorance and heresy Muslims are bound to fight such evils and finish them by means of jihad.* **390 `Abdullah bin `Umar**

A question concerning aHadith was asked on the site **IslamQ&A**: [86]

Q: Why do we have to follow the aHadith of the Prophet Mohammad and not just follow the Quran?

A:

a) *Allah says: "He who obeys the Messenger has indeed obeyed Allah..." [al-Nisaa' 4:80]*
b) *Allah has made obedience to His Prophet a religious duty; resisting or opposing it is a sign of hypocrisy: [al-Nisaa' 4:65]*

If Not This Generation, When?

> *At the heart of this tragedy is a conflict between the first and subsequent generations of British Pakistanis.* (Allah, Liberty and Love, p.146)

When it comes to "subsequent generations", what precisely is the Professor implying? For how many future generations will Pakistanis be Pakistani and not British, Canadian or Western? Right-wingers suggest that this is a classic fifth column.

Dr. Ed Husain, an ex-jihadist who now directs a counter-terrorism center in London:

> *Nobody had the courage to stand up for Liberal democracy when I was a child in school.* (Allah, Liberty and Love, p.153)

Professor Manji does not address why Dr. Husain expects teachers should have courage. In the recent past it was assumed that policemen, firemen, and soldiers needed courage.

---

86 **https://islamqa.info/en/answers/604/justification-for-following-the-sunnah**

Dr. Husain did not tell us why Western values are not adopted by Muslims emigrating to the West. As for "not standing up for democracy," consider what happened to the office of Charlie Hebdo, Salman Rushdie, Molly Norris, cartoonists in Holland, Theo Van Gogh, Samuel Paty and Pim Fortuyn. All stood up for democracy. Some were beheaded, others shot or stabbed, others placed on a death list. Those that carried out the executions are hailed by some in the Muslim community as heroes.

Islamophobes and Right-wingers say Ed Husain is a con man that makes a comfortable living as an ex-jihadist. It is pointed out that Husain, like all reformers, talks about an Islam that could be if only Western governments spent more money on Muslim deradicalization interfaith dialogue programs.

> *Abdul Gaffer Khan never set foot in Europe or America, yet he epitomized universal values that Muslims, including the tens of millions who live in the west can identify with through and through. Countercultural Muslims are his heirs. We are waging the next stage of the struggle to interpret Islam.* (Allah, Liberty and Love, p.154)

Some people have said that with every struggle, there is collateral damage. When men fight in your living room your furniture gets broken. Some will advise you "do not bring this fight into your home". The Right-wing ask why we brought Islam into our home.

Islamophobes say Muslim reformers are not guaranteed victory; nor are they, in that toxic masculine fashion, guaranteeing a victory. Dr. Jasser and Professor Manji have accepted that they are the ones pushing a piano up a hill. Mainstream Islam's sails are full of wind. When is it appropriate to consider the possibility that an Islamic caliphate could be established in certain areas of the West? Is there a point at which it is appropriate to officially acknowledge that Liberal Muslim reformers are losing or have lost? For equity's sake we must ask this question from the inverse. When is it appropriate to consider that mainstream Muslim fundamentalists are winning or have won?

More Apostasy Misunderstanding

> *I wrote that the Quran points out there will always be non-believers, and that it is for God, not us Muslims, to deal with them. Moreover, the Quran bluntly opposes compulsion in religion* (Allah, Liberty and Love, p.161)

Professor Manji is correct – the Quran (and by extension, Allah) does point out there will always be non-believers, but Manji leaves out the fact that Allah says disbelievers are a reviled enemy who must be punished for their disbelief. Allah at times uses his slaves, those who have submitted to him, to enforce his will. The following will add context to the Professor's assertion:

Holy Quran translated by Abdullah Yousif Ali, Lahore, Pakistan, 1934:

> *02:90 ...as for the disbeliever is a humiliating punishment.*
> *02:98 ...Lo! Allah is an enemy of those who reject faith.*
> *02:99 ...none reject faith but those who are perverse.*
> *03:10 Those who reject faith are but fuel for the fire.*

03:50 Those who reject faith, I will punish them with a terrible agony in this world and in the Hereafter.

03:86 Those who reject faith after they have accepted: on them is the curse of Allah, his Angels and all mankind.

03:151 Soon We will cast terror into the hearts of the Unbelievers.

04:56 Those who reject our signs, We will cast into the fire as often as their skins are roasted through.

07:182 Those who reject our signs We shall gradually visit with punishments in ways they perceive not.

09:05... then kill the polytheists wherever you find them.

08:12 I will instill terror into the heart of the Unbeliever: You cut off their heads and their fingertips.

09:33 ...the religion of truth to manifest it over all other religion even though they dislike it.

09:68 Allah has promised the hypocrites and rejecters of Faith the Fire of Hell... For them is the curse of Allah and an enduring punishment.

21:06_As to those before them not one of the populations We destroyed believed; will these believe?

Is it possible that Professor Manji did not read these versus in the Quran? Or perhaps with proper contextualization these verses or sentences could mean something other than what they seem to mean. However: *03:07_The Koran in it are verses basic of established meaning.* In the least, these verses bring into question the Professor's assertion that "the Quran bluntly opposes compulsion in religion." As for "and that it is for God, not us

Muslims, to deal with them," it is understood that Allah can use his servants to mete out punishment:

> *9.14: Fight them, and Allah will punish them by your hands, cover them with shame, help you [to victory] over them.*

Imam Suleiman Bengharsa agrees with Professor Manji insomuch that you cannot force people to believe:

> *You cannot force someone to believe, but you can force them to live under the Shari'ah. Under the Shari'ah, conditions are so difficult that non-Muslims may decide to become Muslim.* [87]

Imam Bengharsa is referring to the Pact of Umar. Earlier in this book, we learned from Professor Manji that this pact is more than doctrine but has attained the status of Holy Scripture. The Professor implies that she is not in favor of this pact and the way it codifies the "mistreatment" of non-Muslims. The Pact of Umar reflects the verses and the comments of the Imam provided above. The Quran is believed to be the literal word of Allah; it follows that the sentiments expressed in the verses are those of Allah. Islamophobes take it further and say, therefore destroying and terrorizing non-believers is the will of Allah.

Mainstream Muslim leaders have clearly and unequivocally stated that Islam is against mistreatment. Is coercing women to wear the burqa mistreatment or a sign of respecting their honour and chastity? Some believe that beating a female for leaving the house without prior authorization is mistreatment.

---

87 *ttps://youtu.be/URqm7p97nBA*

But are beating, stoning, clitoris modifying and hand amputating mistreatment? Depending on perspective and contextualization, there is diversity of opinions on this matter.

Bolstering the Will of Allah

There are many influential senior Imams and scholars past and present who advocate wiping out disbelief using jihad. Is this a misrepresentation of the true meaning of jihad?

The following is taken from *Garden of the Righteous*:

> *Wherever in the world there is tyranny, ignorance and heresy, Muslims are bound to fight such evils and finish them by means of jihad.*
>
> *The objective of jihad... warrants that one must struggle against kufr (disbelief) and shirk polytheism and the worship of falsehood in all its forms... Jihad has to continue until this objective is achieved... The jihad will continue till the day of resurrection...*
>
> *It is incumbent on the Muslims to wage jihad against them to wipe out kufr (disbelief) and shirk polytheism and raise the banner of oneness of God everywhere... This Hadith strongly refutes those people who distort the Islamic concept of jihad and hold that Islam preaches defensive war only...* **[Al-Bukhari and Muslim].**

It is important to note that the above teachings are preached and readily available in mosques and Muslim book- stores across the world. Some will say these teachings are historic and no longer relevant to the Islam of today.

In summer 2018, **Sheikh Karim AbuZaid** gave a weekend workshop at Salaheddin Islamic Centre in Scarborough, Ontario on the book *Islamic Guidelines for Individual & Social Reform* by Sheikh Muhammad bin Jamil Zino. The following excerpts are from the book:

> *Jihad fighting in the cause of Allah: Jihad is obligatory on every Muslim in two ways: by spending one's wealth or offering one's self for fighting in the cause of Allah.*
>
> *For example, propagation of Islam or call to Islam until all countries embrace it and make [Islam] their way of life.*

Professor Manji tell us something that seems to conflict.

> *The Quran also advises we remain open towards the offenders. Pack up in peace, then pick up the conversation when the dust settles.* (Allah, Liberty and Love, p.162)

It would be helpful if the Professor would cite the chapter and verse she is referring to. As far as I know, this idea or concept is not found in the Quran or any Islamic doctrine. However, there is a story in the New Testament involving shaking the dust off your feet/ sandals. This could explain the Professor's confusion.

> *When ye depart out of that house or city, shake off the dust of your feet.* (Matthew 10:11–15) (Mark 6:10–11). (Luke 9:4–5).

The Hijab Can Be Political

> *Some women tell me by choosing the hijab they make a political point, not a spiritual world one.* (Allah, Liberty and Love, p.181)

Imam Syed Rizvi: *The hijab is a female's form of jihad.*[88]

There is a debate in Quebec and Europe concerning the hijab or face veil that revolves around the concept of religious accommodation. All human rights legislation from the UN down, including human rights tribunals in Canada, do not make accommodations for political statements. People considered Islamophobic have argued that Muslims under the guise of religious freedom are making a political play. This is commonly referred to as creeping Shari'ah.

Right-wingers in Canada are trying to propagate the idea that official multiculturalism has gone too far. They say it is being used as a weapon by Islamists. Those on the left say this is nonsense and that such an idea in and of itself should not be tolerated, and that questioning diversity could lead to anti-diversity sentiment, which leads to hate speech.

Those on the right respond: In 2010, the Canadian Broadcast Corporation reported on a Muslim female who was being disruptive in her many demands. She was expelled from her government language class because she insisted it was her religious right to deliver an oral presentation with her back to the class. [89]

---

88 https://youtu.be/Fbdi4pHiIpo

89 https://www.cbc.ca/news/canada/montreal/quebec-to-address-niqab-issue-1.899729

Morgan Lowrie, *The Canadian Press* (Oct 22, 2017)

Quebec Muslim women discuss the banning religious symbols bill:

> *My niqab is my portable curtain.* Naili, 34, said in an interview near her home in Montreal.
>
> *I can go everywhere and be reached and reach people as I want.*
>
> *Fatima Ahmad, a 21-year-old Montreal university student, said she felt compelled to begin wearing the niqab just over a year ago, during the month of Ramadan. "I want to control who I give the permission to access my body," she said. "I think every woman, and every person, should have this right."* [90]

Some Quebecers see this as the slow but steady Islamization of Quebec society. NCCM does advocate turning Montreal into an Islamic enclave.

Professor Manji says that the teacher could have instructed the Muslim woman on the "proper" understanding of Islam as a religion that can be flexible and accommodating. The Professor tells us the teacher should have said, "I know there are passages in the Quran that allow you to take off your niqab." Perhaps the Muslim woman does not want to take off her niqab because, as Imam Syed Rizvi said, wearing the hijab is the female form of jihad. Furthermore, why should the teacher and the other students be drawn into a debate about Islam in a language class? That would be disruptive. Right-wingers and Islamophobes say being disruptive is the point.

90 *https://nationalpost.com/news/canada/quebec-women-whove-worn-niqabs-discuss-provinces-controversial-neutrality-bill*

Halloween Face Mask

Some Feminist groups argue that erasing women's identity from the public sphere is misogyny. Right-wingers argue that those who wear a disguise as a matter of principle are acting with disdain and contempt. Since the beginning of time, people have seen the face of their fellow people.

Reformist Muslims do not wear the veil and are trying to eliminate this practice. It must be noted that the veil is seen as the ultimate and final barrier to the sin of fornication. Some Imams have ruled that when a woman is well beyond child-bearing age and no longer desirable she can unveil.

NCCM offers workshops to school boards, human rights organizations and Muslim advocacy organizations on how to use the media to normalize hijabs and create the view that the hijab, veil and Islam are a champion of human rights.

Islamophobes argue this is evidence that the hijab is not about spirituality but an identity marker to make a clear distinction between us and them. This is a form of "otherizing." They reference Toronto senior Imam Syed Rizvi and Imam Shabbir Ally.

Imam Syed Rizvi:

> *Muslim women are being targeted because they practice their faith, they are actually not only doing something on a personal level to practice this faith,* ***it is in a way jihad for them.*** **Muslim men, we can just go around because [the] beard is very common in many cultures. Attire-wise, there is no issue.** *It is the hijab which is the distinctive identity* **of Muslim women.** [91]

91 https://youtu.be/Fbdi4pHiIpo

Imam Shabbir Ally:

> *The other verse in question is in the 33rd chapter the 59th verse which says: 'Tell the believing women draw a part of their outer garments around themselves, or close to themselves, so that they will be recognized and not molested'…."*[92] *November 2020*

Is it inappropriate to ask if other cultural accommodation such as the wearing of the niqab during a citizenship ceremony is an act of jihad? Islamophobes say that hiding your face during a citizenship ceremony is an act of contempt. According to them, Muslims are saying, "You will grant us citizenship and we will benefit from all the perks that it entails, but we will do it on our terms. You will capitulate to us." Human rights groups disagree with this statement.

Professor Manji tells us the story of a man she met on her book promotion tour. He told her that he donated money to the building of a mosque. She asked him what he knew about the leadership, what strand of Islam would be preached from the mosque. He told her he knew nothing. He helped build this mosque because Islamophobes and Right-wingers were against building the mosque. (Allah, Liberty and Love, p.190).

It follows then that some could be against Islam only because people they do not like are pro-Islam.

Death to Rushdie

During her travels across America on 10 September 2001, Professor Manji found herself at the Houston Theater, where three hundred people were shouting "Death to Rushdie." (Allah, Liberty and Love, p.191) She goes on to say that a man who said he was affiliated with

92 *https://youtu.be/Da6ZM1YWHI*

the Houston Islamic Education Center said the Ayatollah's fatwa against Rushdie was valid. This is significant because this mosque's website states it is directly connected to hundreds of mosques and charities across the Western world: [93]

> *The Islamic Education Center of Houston serves the community as a center for the Friday congregation, Islamic celebrations, community programs, and above all – a center for imparting knowledge about Islam and promoting Islamic values.*

This mosque is oriented to preserving and promoting Islam from preschool to grade twelve:

> *OUR GOALS: Facilitate students' learning of Islamic history, beliefs, morals and jurisprudence. Utilize modern teaching strategies and techniques to help students achieve attainable goals in understanding Islamic teachings and implementing them into their lives.*

This endeavor to educate children to reflect the values and morals of Islam is the same goal as that of the Green Dome in the province of Alberta. Are Muslim schools across North America, Europe and Australia teaching a reformed progressive liberal Islam? According to a member of this mosque, this community supports the fatwa to kill Salmon Rushdie.

Canadian Imam Syed Hassan Mujtaba Rizvi:

> *But when I look towards Allah and I see that he has [an] affiliation with Iran, has no affiliations with Canada, with America, I say* ***I have affiliations with Iran****.*

---

93 https://iec-houston.org/sunday-school/

Speech on the streets of Toronto:

> *You have to know this is not going to stop. It is only the beginning and as it goes forward these are the steps of the one government that is* ***going to be over the whole world*** *and that is the government of the time of the One Imam.*

Speech at the protest of Innocents of Muslims:

> *We will stand, as we stood today, as we will stand in the future, for any insult to the Prophet. And you should know this is going to continue, it will not stop. As God is our witness, we will see the day when [the]* ***religion of Allah will rule over all the oppressors*** *and justice and peace will rule the world.*

Imam Abdula Obeid's speech at a rally in Ottawa**:**

> *All people, Canadians, and all people around the world, are going to say, 'Oh the one who follows the path of the family of Mohammad,' meaning they will accept his authority…*

Toronto Imam Mazin Adhim:

> *Our loyalty is to the Khilafah, if it exists and to the Khalifa if it doesn't exist. Our vision of what the Khalifa is, and what we are working towards, remains, and it's going to be re-established, Allah willing. And our loyalty must remain with it, whether it's present or absent, because this is the only thing we are allowed to have loyalty towards, the full implementation of Islam.*[94]

94 *https://youtu.be/WIPoFdr-rGE*

Death by Stoning Contextualized

Many say stoning people to death should be stopped. Professor Manji is calling for an urgent debate on the issue. She compares the Muslim act of stoning to the Christian act of burning at the stake. Burning at the stake in not found in any Christian doctrine.

Stoning is readily found in Islamic doctrine. According to Hadith categorized as saheeh, Prophet Mohammad *PBUH* ordered a pregnant woman be stoned to death. He ordered that the stoning take place after the child had been weaned. Mohammad *PBUH,* said funeral prayers over the dead woman. Muslims understand this Hadith demonstrates the Prophet's kindness and compassion. **(Book 017, 4206)**

Leaders of the Islamic community contend that eliminating the practice of stoning will do a disservice to Muslims by preventing admittance to paradise. The following from **Toronto Imam Faisal Abdur-Razak,** author of *The Book of Death* helps us understand the benefits of stoning: [95]

> *If someone commits certain crimes in Islam and is found guilty by an Islamic Court, one of the punishments is stoning to death. But for the believer, there is an important benefit. This act of stoning now is also purification for the believer.*

Stoning is integral to the culture and religion of Islam. Canada guarantees cultural and religious rights. Some argue Canadian society should, at a minimum, accept the validity of stoning on a conceptual, symbolic basis as integral to Muslims and Islam. Some claim that to

95 *https://youtu.be/ju_i63myQx4*

deride stoning as barbaric and cruel is an insult to the religion of Islam, the Muslim community and Prophet Mohammad *PBUH.*

Islamophobes, Right-wingers and Muslim reformers, argue that stoning is cruel and barbaric and should be denounced as such in no uncertain terms.

International speaker and scholar Tarik Ramadan is calling for a nuanced approach. He has stated that any attempt to categorically ban stoning would be seen as an attack against Islam and the Prophet Mohammad *PBUH*. He advises a temporary moratorium. [96]

Is Killing Yourself for Allah Suicide?

> *Qatari based theologian Yusuf al-Qaradawi came to endorse suicide bombings of Israeli civilians. The Quran expressly opposes suicide under all pretexts and employs Muslim combatants to have mercy on non-combatants.* (Allah, Liberty and Love, p.197)

It is true that Islam forbids suicide. But when we hear of or experience Muslim suicide, it is not a depressed man ending his life in a basement. We will unpack the second assertion of Professor Manji's statement first. "...have mercy to non-combatants." – If someone did not actively impede a marching army, could they be deemed a combatant? If someone who has been invited to join Islam refuses, are they to be considered a combatant? If someone openly apostatizes or insults Islam, are they a combatant?

---

96 https://tariqramadan.com/an-international-call-for-moratorium-on-corporal-punishment-stoning-and-the-death-penalty-in-the-islamic-world/

Islamic leaders and doctrine do encourage sacrificing the life of this world for the cause of Allah. Similarly, a Japanese kamikaze pilot was not considered to be committing suicide when he flew his plane into the enemy.

According to *The Clear Quran,* by **Canadian Imam Dr. Mustafa Khattab**:

> *29:64 This worldly life is no more than play and amusement. But the hereafter is indeed the real life if only they knew.*
>
> *2:154 Never say that those martyred in the cause of Allah are dead – in fact, they are alive! But you do not perceive it.*

Muslim scholars and clerics explain how those alive in Paradise live.

Toronto Imam Syed Regeah:

> *You can only find the black-eyed virgins in Paradise... Allah said about men who go to Paradise: We give them wives from the black-eyed virgins of Paradise.*

Ammadiyya Muslim website:

> *Female companions of exceeding beauty and refinement would be provided to the pious men with no limit imposed on the number, which will be decided according to their capacity.*
>
> *[In] the lowest level in Jannah (Paradise) a man will be married to two black-eyed virgins and in the highest he gets 72 virgins...*

Saudi cleric and Sheikh Muhammad Ali Shanghili:

> *Every Muslim man gets at least two black-eyed virgins in Paradise. Each virgin comes with 70 servant girls; you are permitted to have sex with the servant girls as well.*

Saudi Sheikh Yahya Al Jana:

> *The breasts of the virgins of Paradise are like pomegranates, they don't sag. They are beautiful. Allah even mentioned sex, in order to make you lust for Paradise. It is not just food, drink, and happiness. Allah said, "The dwellers of Paradise are busy." What keeps them busy? They will be busy tearing hymens. Prophet Mohammad PBUH said: "By Allah, a man will have a hundred virgins in a single morning." What is even more amazing is that each time he returns to one of them, he will find that she is a virgin again, not like the women of this world. The dwellers of Paradise will be given the strength of a hundred men when it comes to eating, drinking and sex.* [97]

It is hard to imagine that any Muslim is unaware of these Islamic teachings that add important context to the topic of Muslim suicide jihad. This helps us understand why there will always be a cohort of young men eager to sacrifice themselves for the cause of social justice, equity, peace and Allah *SWT.*

Contextualizing Hate in the Quran

> *Frankly, I'm not certain that all pugnacious verses of the Quran can be reinterpreted for our century.* (Allah, Liberty and Love, p.222)

Professor Manji says the Quran contains verses that are quarrelsome and combative. Therefore, she is also saying that Islam is a quarrelsome and combative religion. Let's assume that

97 *https://youtu.be/8sxkjSRZBec*

somewhere in the Quran we can find loving, compassionate verses, as reformer Raheel Raza and many others tell us are there. That will not stop Muslims from acting upon the "pugnacious" verses. When Muslims act upon said verses, are they to be considered good or bad Muslims?

8:39 And fight them till all religion is only for Allah.

2:191 Kill them wherever you find them.

It is also possible that with the proper contextualization these words could be interpreted to mean something other than what they plainly seem to mean. In the past and certainly in the future, misunderstanding Muslims have and will act upon these words in a manner that is not contextualized.

We must not lose sight of the fact that after every Muslim jihadist attack, Muslim associations and politicians make a statement. Some say issuing statements does not stop Muslim jihadists from misunderstanding and attacking. This brings us back to the beginning. It is not about right and wrong, true or false. It is about the fundamental right of the Muslim Ummah to live and express their sincere religious belief.

> *Any gesture, including a humanitarian one, can be interpreted as hostile to Islam depending on the political agenda.* (Allah, Liberty and Love, p.227)

Is Professor Manji telling us that Muslim leaders could on any pretext interpret hostility and instigate a riot if it serves their agenda? The Danish cartoons are one example.

Early in 2009, the UKIP peer Lord Pearson of Rannoch of the House of Lords, invited the Dutch politician Geert Wilders to a private meeting in the Palace of Westminster. He had intended to invite his colleagues in the Lords to a private viewing of the documentary *Fitna*, followed by discussion and debate. Lord Ahmed issued a threat that he would personally mobilize ten thousand Muslims to prevent Wilders from entering the upper house and take the peer organizing the event to court. In the face of such threats, the meeting was canceled. Lord Ahmed is considered to be a "moderate" Muslim. Pakistan-born Nazir Ahmed became the United Kingdom's first Muslim life peer in 1998, appointed by Tony Blair.

"Moderate" is Extreme When Compared to "Mild"

> *I recommend when discussing Islam with moderates, the question goes like this: "I'm not wondering about the theory of Islam, which I trust is beautiful. But I am wondering about the practice of it. What elements of Islam, when followed in the real and imperfect world, lead to pain – and why? It is a question designed to cut through the third tendency: that the moderates talk about Islam in the abstract. This tendency breeds banalities such as "Islam is peace." When skeptics hear that cliché, they often take it as a sign of Muslim duplicity.* (Allah, Liberty and Love, *p.227)*

Professor Manji is telling us that in the practical sense Islam is a religion that brings pain, and that moderate Muslims ignore realities by focusing on the abstract. She also tells us the phrase "Islam is peace," often repeated by moderates, is interpreted by skeptics to be a cliché designed to create a smoke screen.

> *Muslims are fearful because by asking these things, we may be forsaking our religion. But why must the choice be losing or keeping our religion? Why not a third choice: transforming our understanding of religion by reforming ourselves.* (Battle Soul Islam)

Manji advocates a third choice, but Islamic leaders and doctrine do not allow for a third choice. Islam divides the world in two – those who are Muslim and those who are not.

> ***280 Mu'adh** reported that Messenger of Allah (PBUH) sent me (as a governor of Yemen) and instructed me thus: "You will go to the people of the Book. First call them to testify that there is no true god except Allah **[Al-Bukhari and Muslim]**.*
>
> *Commentary:*
>
> *l. If it comes to Jihad against infidels, polytheists and the people of the Book **(Ahl-ul-Hitab)** then before waging war against them, they should be invited to Islam.*

"Transforming our understanding of religion by reforming ourselves." How will transforming "ourselves" reform the mainstream Muslim community that is hostile to reform?

Those that exited the Ariana Grande concert or completed the Boston Marathon or the parents of Lee Rigby or… might not be open to the idea of transforming their understanding.

CHAPTER 13

ISLAMIC CALIPHATE — MYTH OR FACT?

In this chapter we explore how Western governments embrace the development of areas that promote Muslim culture. We also explore how Islamophobes interpret this as an attempt to establish a parallel Muslim society.

Thorncliffe Park in Toronto is a large crescent which does not contain houses, but massive apartment blocks. The population of twenty thousand is 95% Muslim. Many of the women wear the full burqa, Taliban, ISIS style. Thorncliffe Park contains a madrassa and a mosque/community center.

In August 2021, Ed Husain of London, UK, was interviewed about his book *Among the Mosques: A Journey Across Muslim Britain*:

> *Combined with communalism and clericalism, what unites both of these factors is the third factor, which you see in book publications, which you see in events. It is this; Caliphism – the belief that somehow, someday a caliphate will emerge somewhere*

> *again. In other words, a Muslim supremacist empire. On the Muslim far right you have this constant demand for the return of the caliphate. There is this strong idea of a Shari'ah-dominant clerical communal home, i.e. a caliphate. It is a real issue. For those who doubt me, I refer you to the 42,000 individuals who are subjects of interest for the intelligence services. Why? It is because they believe in creating a caliphate. In the absence of doing it in the Middle East, they create these little communal caliphates in Doonesbury and parts of Blackburn, Rochdale, Leeds, Manchester and Birmingham.* [98]

As of 2011, 61% of all Muslims in Canada live in Ontario – that is 580,000 people, or 4.6% of the Ontario population[99] Quebec has 240,000 Muslims, representing 3.2% of the total population. In this book we have learned that Imams and Muslim leaders encourage Muslims to consolidate forces in an effort to more effectively lobby for Islam and the establishment of Shari'ah. The religion of Islam supersedes the boundaries of nation states. As children, Muslims are told that their loyalty is to Islam and the *Ummah* (global Muslim community). Many Muslims are taught that dying to further the cause of Allah will guarantee their entry into Paradise.

In a Global Village, All Villages Are the Same

In France, there are 751 areas the government officially calls *zones urbaines sensibles* (sensitive urban zones), or ZUS, for short. Police

98 *https://youtu.be/RAXDniO11l4*

99 https://www.worldatlas.com/articles/canadian-provinces-and-territories-by-muslim-population.html

will only enter with significant backup. The average ZUS contains about six thousand residents. An estimated five million people live in these zones, and virtually all are Muslim. In some zones, Shari'ah supersedes the French legal system on civil matters such as property disputes, adultery and divorce. [100] [101]

> Dr. Ed Husain says that many Muslims in Britain are living in "another universe" in which "Taliban-esque" cultural norms are enforced. He says half of the mosques in the United Kingdom were established by Deobandis, who were responsible for the creation of the Taliban in Afghanistan. This cultural diversity has also enriched other European countries. For that matter, all that we consider to be Western civilization, including Latin America, is also being enriched. [102]

60 Minutes Sweden's Cultural Insensitivity

Three white people, - two men and a woman - entered the Muslim Somali area of Rinkaby, Sweden. They did this without prior authorization. The woman was not wearing a hijab and was exposing her blonde hair. This alone was seen as an affront to the cultural values of Islam. When you couple that with the fact that they had a camera, well…

---

100 https://www.foxnews.com/world/paris-attacks-prompt-fears-frances-muslim-no-go-zones-incubating-jihad

101 https://www.breitbart.com/europe/2021/06/06/no-go-zones-for-white-people-in-britain-muslim-author-documents/

102 https://sencanada.ca/en/Content/Sen/committee/412/secd/51874-e

Welcome back to 60 Minutes. *I have just returned from Sweden where something happened...*

Within minutes of their police escort leaving, the men were physically attacked. The attack, however, was not brutal.

> *I never would have imagined in such a wonderful country...*

Sweden has been dramatically altered since its fateful decision in 2015 to open its doors to refugees from Syria, Afghanistan and Iraq. They have since seen many things that were previously considered unimaginable, such as gangs using grenades, or areas were police are attacked by mobs.

> *Unfortunately, Sweden has become a victim of its own humanity. By opening its doors and welcoming hundreds of thousands of refugees and asylum seekers, the country is experiencing serious security issues – and it's not alone.* [103]

Before the 2015 refugee crisis, there were approximately six hundred thousand Muslims in Sweden. [104]As of 2017, the Muslim community is 810,000, or 8.1% of the total population. In September 2022, a study updated from 2015 names 61 zones where crime has significantly spiked. The report also says that those living in these zones are vulnerable to religious radicalization.

Sweden has witnessed a surge in Islamist extremists: from two hundred a decade ago to "thousands" in 2017, according to the Scandinavian country's spies chief. Police believe five thousand criminals and two hundred criminal networks are based across the 61 areas.

---

103 https://youtu.be/vO9vBHZRBQ4

104 https://en.wikipedia.org/wiki/United_States_Department_of_State

Everyone in these zones is a Muslim. [105] Statistics tells us that only a minority are willing and capable of carrying out an attack on Swedish soil. Thornberg said some Swedish national security threats may not be detectable, as militants no longer need months to prepare for a high-tech assault

> *We have never seen anything like this before, this is the 'new normal'... It is a historic challenge that extremist circles are growing. Today, you buy two knives or hire a truck and drive into a crowd.*

Such incidents are not confined to Sweden. Right-wing political parties in Europe exploited the 2016 New Year's Eve celebration. They cite mainstream media reports about mass sexual assaults at Germany's Cologne train station.

Huffington Post:

> *Security forces were unable to get all of the incidents, assaults, crimes, etc. under control. There were simply too many happening at the same time. Officials were overwhelmed and powerless to help some people calling for help. Groups of male migrants were repeatedly named as perpetrators.*

Police officers were "bombarded with fireworks and pelted with glass bottles." [106]

---

105 https://www.newsweek.com/sweden-sees-influx-thousands-islamist-extremists-spy-chief-says-626581

106 https://www.huffpost.com/entry/cologne-train-station-attacks_n_568e88b7e4b0cad15e639ee2

Many are hoping that that the Muslim reform movement will counter this phenomenon of growing Islamism in Europe, North America and Australia. Professor Manji did tell us about an Arab Israeli in Germany with the **Liberal Muslim Empowerment Network.** This network is helping Muslims redefine honour. We can assume that such networks are also being started in other European countries.

Globalization Brings What Is Over There Over Here

Academics and most Western governments agree globalization will replace individual national cultures with a global super culture. Some ask if creating mini Islamic zones in the West is a cultural benefit of globalization.

CHAPTER 14

THE COUNTER-REFORM MOVEMENT

In this chapter we will appreciate that, for every move Muslim reformers make to liberalize Islam, mainstream Muslims make a counter-move. We will learn how the interplay between Reformers and Fundamentalists define a civilization and its perception toward women, democracy/free speech, art and music.

Spy vs. Spy… Reformer vs. Fundamentalist…

What are the counter-moves to the reform movement? In Canada, NCCM's CEO Mustafa Farooq is encouraging Muslims to create mini Islamic states in Edmonton, Montreal and Ottawa. He also heads a campaign that promotes Islam and the hijab as a champion of human rights. CCI also promotes the teaching that it is the religious duty of Muslims to strive in implementing Shari'ah. The MSA (Muslim Student Association) has a chapter in every North American university. This organization is incrementally and consistently advances the Islamic narrative of peace, justice and total submission to Allah since 1965.[107]

On February 23-27 2015, the MSA held their annual Islam Awareness Week on the campus of York University in Toronto under the title "What Does the Qur'an Say?"

Pious Muslim female students, completely covered with thick black cloth, Taliban/ISIS style, manned the dawa'h booth at the Central Square of York University and handed out copies of the book *Women in Islam & Refutation of Common Misconceptions*, written by Saudi scholar Dr. Abdul Rahman al-Sheha and printed by the Muslim World League, a Saudi organization dedicated to propagating Islam throughout the world.

This book is also distributed by the Islamic dawa'h team at Toronto Dundas Square. It helps us contextualize the dynamic interplay that takes place when Western and Muslim cultures intersect. The book *Women in Islam* tells us secular laws do not give the Muslim community Islamic justice:

> *If the Islamic laws were established and executed, the severe punishments for fornication, adultery, murder, etc., would satisfy the Muslim population that justice has been done, and this would curtail the sense of vengeance that one needs to have recourse to...*

Women in Islam also instructs Muslim men on the proper methodology to employ when beating females, including their wives:

107 http://www.ihistory.co/first-muslim-students-association/

Third and final stage: Beating without hurting, breaking a bone, leaving black or blue marks on the body, and avoiding hitting the face or especially sensitive places at any cost. The purpose of beating her is only to discipline. Islam forbids severe beating as punishment. The Prophet PBUH said: "None of you should beat his wife like a slave-beating and then have intercourse with her at the end of the day.

This treatment is proved to be very effective with two types of women: strong-willed, demanding and commandeering women. Also, submissive or subdued women may even enjoy being beaten at times as a sign of love and concern. [Bukhari #4908]

Some have said that distributing a book that advocates beating women is a perversion of what Dr. Jasser calls "my Islam." This however does not change the fact that this message of beating women is being propagated by women in universities across North America.

On January 22, 2019, the MSA at York University posted the following on its official Facebook page:[108]

Asalamualaykum! We have updated our constitution.

*2. **Objectives:***

2.01 The MSA is a mainstream Sunni Islamic Association that follows and adheres to the Qur'an and Sunnah upon the understanding of the Salaf.

2.02 The MSA will organize events in accordance with the Shari'ah. Any innovations in religious matters or

108 https://news.acdemocracy.org/york-msas-constitution-spreading-the-teachings-of-islam-on-campus/

"modernization" will not be acceptable, as Islam is a way of life for all times and places and hence is not subject to being outdated or needing reform.

Women Protecting the Image of Islam

Professor Manji told us she is developing a task force of Muslim reformers in Europe to respond quickly to future Muslim terror attacks with messages of love and compassion. This will ensure the image of Islam is not besmirched. Some say this is propaganda designed to whitewash the reality that terrorism is a fundamental tool used by Islam.

In Toronto, several women's groups came together to defend the image of Islam. In the article "Girl Interrupted," Mary Rogan discusses the concept of sensitivity to multiculturalism and whether it led to the death of Aqsa Parvez. Mary Rogan labeled the strangulation of Aqsa Parvez by her brother and father as an honour killing, which upset the Muslim community and a number of feminist groups.

Mary Rogan:

There were online debates and ugly postings saying that the conclusions I had drawn, even if they weren't wrong... were racist, and this story was another example of the growing persecution of Muslims in North America. [109]

109 https://torontolife.com/city/revisiting-aqsa-parvez-qa-with-mary-rogan/

The women's groups uploaded seven minutes of a symposium to YouTube. In it they defended the reputation of Islam, denounced Canada, the article and the editor of the publication.[110]

The following is a transcript:

Michelle Cho – Urban Alliance on Race Relations:

When I read Toronto Life's *feature "Girl Interrupted," I was outraged. While Aqsa Parvez has not been forgotten, I am dismayed by the way she is being remembered, and how her death has been sensationalized to further anti-immigration, Islamophobic and racist rhetoric. This is irresponsible journalism and only polarizes the issues and our community. This article feeds into fear-mongering driven by us-versus-them mentality, suggesting that embracing diversity is like a runaway train leading to the death of Western liberalism as we know it. This article makes the suggestion that multiculturalism has gone too far and this is simply offensive. It assumes that violence is linked to one culture and religion rather than the fact that an individual's criminal behavior is supported by a society that refuses to acknowledge the larger context of violence against women in our country ...*

To focus on cultural differences or try to point to the imagined incendiary nature of what is a peaceful religion is to actually take away attention from the tragic fact that a young woman was killed. What needs to be addressed is the crisis in gender violence in this country. Racist thinking that only serves to exacerbate the divisions in our community. I would

110 https://youtu.be/E7v0B0qjgXw

seriously encourage Toronto Life *to examine its commitment to civic journalism in ways that support dialogue, provide an opportunity for more journalists and editors to examine their racial bias, Islamophobia and sexism would help to provide thoughtful and balanced coverage.*

Hellen Johannes:

In relation to the conference today, Islam is being blamed. Canadian systemic factors play a role in violence against women and young women, school institutions, police institutions, government institutions, policies that are made, media outlets; all these are systemic, perpetuate violence, they create stereotypes that are extremely oppressive.

Sumayya Kassamali – Muslims Against Violence:

I tend to avoid speaking about Islam publicly because it is over-tokenized and it is a discussion that comes up too often, and unfairly.

One of the most offensive parts of this article ... really needs to be addressed. The article access story was presented in a particular way. And the easiest way to summarize it I think is to quote. "Aqsa Parvez had a choice: wear the hijab to please her devoted family or take it off and be like her friends. She paid for her decision with her life."

The conclusion of the article is poised to how offensive the representation of Islam ... not only the individual violence against women, but Islam specifically. And the article concludes ... that on a high degree of horror of, the possibility may have

> *feared that her father and her brother were right in their violent demands.*
>
> *And I think we really need to trouble this especially in the country where we say you have freedom of religion, where we say we have respect for Islam and for other cultural and religious diversity. This article really troubles that misconception and shows the underlying Islamophobia of that organization.*

Nuzhat Jafri - Canadian Council of Muslim Women:

> *Muslim women and women generally are tired of being discussed and debated and in particular [about] what they wear. We are really, really tired of this debate. There is no debate. We have the right to choose what we wear, where we live, how we live. There is no one telling us what we must do, or say, or how we dress.*

This last speaker, a hijab-wearing woman, is upset about men telling women what to wear. She makes a bold assertive statement:

> *There is no debate. We have the right to choose what we wear.*

This is a symposium in response to an article about a girl killed by her Muslim father and brother for choosing NOT to wear the hijab. A question that was not addressed is could this strangulation be a warning to Muslim women?

It is understood in Islamic teachings that a male can either grant or deny a female permission to leave the house. However, there is no discussion about males granting females permission to uncover their hair in public.

Vancouver Mufti Aasim Rashid:

> *When [a woman] is granted permission to leave the house, how should she appear? She should be completely covered. The face and hands may be exposed.* [111]

In the opinion of Imam Aasim, the face and hands do not have to be covered. However, on this point there is no *ijma* (consensus). A large minority of Imams and scholars that say covering the face is *fard* (mandatory). Some insist that the hands and eyes be covered as well. In order for a female to see where she is walking, some Imams permit the woman to make small pin holes or have a thinner cloth at the eyes that is somewhat see-through. Some schools of Salif allow for one eye to be completely exposed.

Sheikh Abu Ameenah Bilal Philips:

> *Muslim women who do not wear the hijab are still Muslim. It is not enough to take them out of Islam. But women who do not wear the hijab are living in sin.*

According to the book *Islam: Balancing Life and Beyond,* distributed at Dundas Square in Toronto:

> *Whereas when a woman chooses to show her body in one form or another, the message is only one: she wants attention and possibly much more.*

So then, Nuzhat Jafri from the Canadian Council of Muslim Women is either not a knowledgeable Muslim or she is misrepresenting the religion of Islam, or she wishes to reform Islam. Whichever it is,

---

111 *https://youtu.be/lNKuNKhc0h4*

it is absolutely false to say Muslim women can wear what they want. Technically Muslim women such as Aqsa Parvez and the Shafia Girls did wear what they wanted, but they paid with their lives for a privilege that Western females take for granted. In some Islamic countries, a mob or the Islamic virtue police will do a woman serious harm if she appears in public not properly wearing the hijab or adhering to the concept of hijab.

In Afghanistan today, she is completely covered. Some Muslims will say that the Taliban is an extremist Muslim group that does not represent Islam. All non-Muslims and Muslim reformers will agree with this. But is it true that the Taliban does not represent the true Islam? Colorado Imam Karim AbuZaid in August of 2021 uploaded a lecture in which he said:

> *Now the laws of Taliban – the laws of the Shari'ah – of Islam, that's what they want to implement in their country. So what is wrong with that? Why don't you not place this on the same level,* ***equal to Macron forcing women not to wear their hijab*** *under the notion of keeping the custom and the principles of the Republic? Taliban happen to be the ruling authority in Afghanistan. Don't they have the right to at least show their women the Islamic dress code?*

How does all this interplay with the agenda of the Muslim reformers? We have Muslim students that clearly advocate Sunni Islam. We have a group of both Muslim and non-Muslim women denouncing a magazine that was seemingly critical of the Islamic culture, if not the religion, that led to the death of a sixteen-year-old girl.

In North America, senior Imams openly support the Taliban's dictate on women's dress code.

A large object in motion stays in motion… Mainstream Islam is a large body at 97% of the mass.

Islam Embracing Free Speech and Human Rights

There are two competing narratives concerning free speech in Islam. There is the narrative promoted by Muslim reformers, and that which is understood by mainstream Muslims. Both Dr. Jasser and Professor Manji tell us that Islam is more than compatible with free speech. They have told us that Islam embraces free speech. However, Muslim leaders in North America tell us that the concept of free speech or freedom of conscience is a Western value that is incompatible with the values of Islam.

> *Human Rights in Islam and Common Misconceptions: (distributed by Toronto Dawa'h)*
>
> *Execution, Islam does not treat rejection of Faith as a personal matter. Rejection is a seed of internal Revolution and instigation towards rebellion. Islam only punishes the apostate himself with the simple, direct and very effective deterrent.*

Shaikh Yasir Qadhi:

> *Islam does not come with anything that is irrational, but it does come with things that are supra-rational i.e., rationality does not and cannot have a role to judge whether it is valid or not. It is beyond the scope of the intellect.* [112]

112 https://youtu.be/ceIj9q9QV9I

Imam Karim AbuZaid:

Copy, mimic Mohammad in your life. You eat with your right hand, because he did that. You sleep on your right side, because he did that. You enter the bathroom with your left foot because he did that.

Islamic Dawa'h Center Scarborough Ontario:

Disunity may be a result of forgetting our primary identity. And we must correct Muslims who preach feminism, liberalism, allegiance to national identity over Islam. The latter may be more difficult and may require more courage and effort. Otherwise, we're going to find ourselves with a generation of Islamic feminists' liberals progressive Muslims... perhaps one solution is to teach what it means to be a Muslim, and the beliefs and allegiances associated with our identity.

Sheharyar Sheikh Imam, Islamic society of Kingston Ontario:

I especially want to look at one aspect of the punishment for apostasy. Let Allah be a witness that I am telling the truth. The punishment for apostasy is death. [113]

Hizb-ut-Tahrir:

Common freedoms are in conflict with the laws of Islam. The Muslim is not free in the matter of his belief. If he apostasies from Islam, he is asked to return. If he does not, his punishment is death. The messenger of Allah said whoever changes his deen, kill him. https://www.hizb.org.uk/

113 https://youtu.be/_PtUJNOISSg

Muslims cannot express any opinion that contradicts Islam. Accordingly, he is not allowed to call for the liberation of women or a principle like capitalism or socialism. Muslims are not allowed freedom of opinion which the capitalists call for. [114]

Australian Imam Mohammad Hoblos:
Islam does not mean peace. Islam means submission. It is submission to Allah and His prophet. Those that submit are called Muslims. The more Muslims submit, the more they will find peace in their lives.

Hadith Al Sharifsa bi ta'reef Al Mustafa, 2/1091:
Waging war against Islam is not limited to fighting with weapons; it may be done verbally such as defaming Islam or the prophet, or attacking the Quran, and so on. Waging verbal war against Islam may be worse than waging war with weapons in some cases.

North American Imam Suleiman Bengharsa:
You must make the non-Muslim feel he must become Muslim in order for him to have equal rights. [115]

Imam Mazin Aadhim:
In Islam the system is itjihad through the Quran and the Sunnah. You refer to the only the text of Islam to determine the

114 *https://www.hizb.org.uk/*
115 https://youtu.be/UvWH-kCYBgo

> *law. Only Allah is the legislator and only Allah has the right to determine the laws.... We fundamentally disagree with man legislating his own laws* [116]

116 *https://youtu.be/ENBe607C71E*

CHAPTER 15

CONCLUSION WITH CONFUSION

Many tell us what Islam is and what it is not. That includes the 26-year-old serving coffee at Starbucks, the right-wing blogger, the Facebook fact checker and the next-door neighbor. If you asked these people, as I have, "What do you know about Islam?" they answer, "I went to school with a Muslim," or, "I work with a Muslim."

I respond, "Perhaps I miscommunicated. I am not asking what you know about Muslims. I am asking what you know about the religion of Islam."

They stare blankly for a few moments, gathering their thoughts. They realize this very simple question is a danger. It lays bare the blatant fallacy upon which most narratives about Islam are predicated.

Seeking Clarity

For some reason, when it comes to Islam, everyone has an opinion and often a strong one. Have you ever heard someone say, "I cannot give an opinion about Islam because I am ignorant on the subject?" For that matter, has anyone ever said that about any subject?

Politicians, media and academia tell us that Islam is the most misunderstood religion. We can all agree on this. What is not agreed to is who is misunderstanding.

When it comes to matters of religion, there can be no proof of what is true or false. I can prove water freezes and that ice melts. Matters of religion are based on faith and are therefore never provable. The Quran tells us that Prophet Mohammad *PBUH* flew to Heaven on a winged horse and several times renegotiated with Allah how many times a day Muslims must pray. Did this actually happen? Is it wrong to believe it did happen?

Western Civilization has the Tooth Fairy and Santa Claus. The fact that there is no tooth fairy is not the point. The point is how or what does this idea/concept contribute to childhood development and by extension development of society. Similarly, some have asked, what does the belief in an intergalactic flying Prophet Mohammed *PBUH* contribute to humanity?

Believe Because

Colorado Imam Karim AbuZaid:

> *Belief and implementation. That's what the believer does. This is the whole religion of Islam. That you make 'belief' of the unseen. What is 'belief'? Believe beyond any shadow of doubt.*

> *You're not skeptical and you don't try to use your intellect. We believe even though it doesn't make sense.... Using your intellect may lead you to leave Islam.* [117]

We are told "all cultures and religions are equal." By extension then all interpretations of religion are equal. Islam is equal to Christianity, Buddhism is equal to Judaism, Shia is equal to Sunni. Liberal progressive Islam is equal to conservative fundamentalist Islam.

Non-Muslims prefer the reformed liberal progressive Islam. However, based on equity, social justice and human rights, no one can say that mainstream fundamental, traditional Islam is not entitled to the same tolerance, acceptance and being embraced. After all, all Muslims, by virtue of being Muslim, contribute to diversity which makes us stronger.

The Extremism Scale

On a scale that measures terrorists, ISIS and Al-Qaeda are ten. Muslims that identify as LGBTQ+ are zero. Where then do we place Canadian Imam Younus Kathrada who supports the policies of the Taliban? What about Muslims who want to live under Shari'ah law or the woman that refuses to remove her face veil at the request of a language teacher? How about Mustafa Farooq who called for Muslims to establish mini Islamic states in Edmonton, Montreal and Ottawa, or the Imam that instructs Muslims not to use their intellect, or the Toronto Police Muslim Chaplain who said men can copulate with children.

---

117 https://www.ericbrazau.com/how-thinking-intellectual-thoughts-causes-muslims-to-apostatize/

The Muslims that beheaded Lee Rigby or the two girls in Morocco or the French teacher are ten; the Shafia father, mother and brother who murdered Zainab, Sahar, and Geeti Shafia are ten. The brother and father that strangled Aqsa Parvez for refusing to wear the hijab are ten. The Toronto 19 that planned to set off a truck bomb in downtown Toronto are ten. The two Via Rail bombers planning to sabotage a passenger train are ten. Muslim convert Aaron Driver who planned to bomb a crowd in Toronto is ten. The Muslim convert who shot the soldier at the war memorial in Ottawa then stormed the parliament building is ten. The Muslim who used his car to run down the two soldiers in St. Jean-sur-Richelieu is ten.

How should we treat the Imam that recites Islamic doctrine about Jews being turned into monkeys and pigs or preaches: "O! Muslims there is a Jew hiding behind me. Come and kill him"? Is he four or seven on the scale? It is easy to reject a ten, socially and legally. What percentage of Westerners considers six a matter for concern? But what should or could be done with those that are six on the scale?

Punishing Tomorrow's Crimes Today

The Liberal government of Justin Trudeau wants to introduce preventative arrest and punishment for possible hate speech (Bill C-36). Particular to this bill is that it establishes a reverse onus for the accused. He must prove beyond an unreasonable doubt that he will not commit a hate speech crime in the future. No such onus is placed on returning ISIS fighters or those accused of supporting Islamic terrorism. Is it equitable to treat perpetrators of future hate speech differently from perpetrators of future Muslim jihadist suicide attacks? Bill C-36 does not apply to possible Muslim terrorism.

No to Logical Fallacies.

In pursuit of equity and social justice we must not conflate individual Muslims with the religion of Islam. It is highly prejudicial to judge a Muslim based on their knowledge of Islamic doctrine just as it is prejudicial to judge Islamic doctrine based on knowledge or the actions of one or several Muslims.

According to Dr. Jasser, some books and commentators tell us there is no moderate Islam, and that Islam's true nature is violently opposed to the infidel. Throughout this book, we have seen that there are plenty of Imams in Canada and across the Western world who could be labeled extreme. Dr. Jasser told us "many mosques preach an Islamic extremism that is non-violent but is a precursor" of the Islamic extremism that influenced radicals like Dr. Ed Husain of Britain and American Major Nidal Hasan.

Nothing To Do but Watch It Happen

Countless Muslim jihad attacks have been thwarted in the past 20 years. This takes enormous manpower and money. In 2017, the number of *official extremists* across Britain, France, Belgium and Germany reached 66,000. In 2017, 51 nonprofits in Brussels' migrant district were suspected of having terror links. [118] [119]

In Western society suspected criminals are given the benefit of the doubt. It is the state that bears the burden of proof. In the case of

118 https://www.breitbart.com/europe/2017/03/20/51-nonprofits-brussels-terror-links/

119 https://www.gatestoneinstitute.org/10480/jihadists-europe

jihad terror attacks much of the proof is available after an incident. The majority of jihadist terror attacks in Britain, Germany, Brussels and France were carried out by Muslims that were under surveillance or on the radar.

Maintaining Hope

Ed Husain's real name is Mohammed Mahbub. Husain, by his own account was involved with political Islamic organizations such as the **Jamat-e-Islami**, the **Muslim Brotherhood** and **Hizb ut-Tahrir**. He tells us that he did not participate directly in Islamic jihad terror plots but was a campus recruiter for Hizb ut-Tahrir that, according to him, laid the ideological seeds for much of contemporary Islamism's manifestations in Britain. Where was Dr. Husain on the scale before his conversion to ex-extremist? Would he have been a six or seven? Is that sufficient for an intervention? Obviously it is not, because no one stopped him from propagating Islamic extremism in Britain.

According to his own admission, Dr. Husain was instrumental in establishing the present Muslim jihadist movement in Britain. Today he writes books, gives lectures and assists Western governments in developing deradicalization programs.

Finding Religion

Dr. Ed Husain changed his beliefs, as do some radical misunderstanding Muslims. However, that change can also go the other way. Lackadaisical, pot-smoking Muslims can become very pious. Contrary to popular belief, this is not necessarily a good thing. Indonesian Imam Abu Bakar Bashir was sentenced to fifteen years for giving spiritual guidance to the men that blew up the Bali nightclub. [120]

What will Western civilization be in 150 years? Look around and observe what is ascending and what is descending. Therein lies your answer. However, it goes without saying that no one can be certain. But what we can say with certainty is that the religion of Islam will exponentially increase its contribution to Western civilization. Will that contribution come from liberal, progressive reform Islam or traditional, mainstream, fundamental Islam? Who will you bet on to win this fight?

@@@

120 https://www.abc.net.au/news/2015-11-17/bali-bombing-spiritual-leader-applies-for-judicial-review/6946154

INDEX

D

E

F

G

H

I

J

Manufactured by Amazon.ca
Bolton, ON